Boston's Gardens & Green Spaces

Boston's Gardens & Green Spaces

Meg Muckenhoupt

Union Park Press • Boston

To Jessica,

[signature]

UNION
PARK
PRESS

Union Park Press
Boston, MA 02118
www.unionparkpress.com

Printed in China through Coloraft Ltd., Hong Kong.
First Edition

Library of Congress Control Number: 2009933789
ISBN: 978-1-934598-03-0; 1-934598-03-8

Book and cover design and production by Elizabeth Lawrence.
Cover photo credits, front: Xiao "Sherman" Gong. Back:
(from left to right) Xiao "Sherman" Gong; Xiao "Sherman"
Gong; Patricia King Powers; Patricia King Powers.

To Heath, Jasper, and Benjy,
who like to get outside,
and to Scott,
who has always inspired me.

Contents

Contents cont.

Green Spaces of Greater Boston

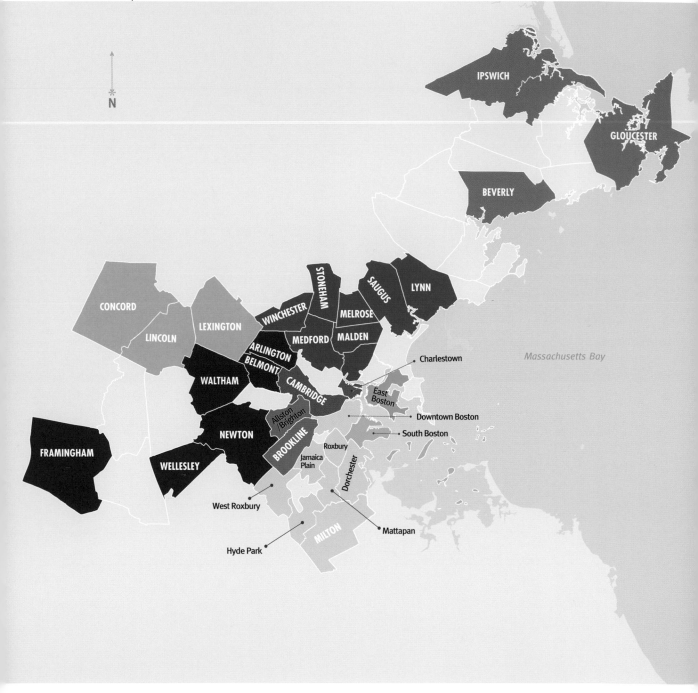

N

IPSWICH

GLOUCESTER

BEVERLY

Massachusetts Bay

CONCORD

LINCOLN

LEXINGTON

WINCHESTER

STONEHAM

SAUGUS

LYNN

MELROSE

MEDFORD

MALDEN

ARLINGTON

BELMONT

WALTHAM

CAMBRIDGE

Charlestown

East
Boston

Downtown Boston

Allston
/Brighton

BROOKLINE

South Boston

FRAMINGHAM

NEWTON

WELLESLEY

Roxbury

Jamaica
Plain

Dorchester

West Roxbury

Mattapan

MILTON

Hyde Park

x

Introduction

BOSTON'S HISTORY IS WRITTEN IN ITS LAND. SINCE THE FIRST bucket of dirt was shoveled into the mud flats off Boston's central Shawmut Peninsula, Bostonians have been building land by the ocean, tearing down hills, re-routing rivers, and creating revolutionary, beautiful, enjoyable green places. Within ten miles of Boston, visitors can explore forests that greeted the first European settlers, stroll the grand nineteenth-century parks of the Emerald Necklace, and experience today's innovative green spaces, including "green roofs," contemporary sculpture parks, healing gardens, and the great blooming swath of the Rose Kennedy Greenway. Boston's vast network of planned and wild open spaces preserves the city's past and reveals its future.

In some ways, the city's green spaces have come full circle. Today's Bostonians have realigned their interest in green spaces with that of earlier Bostonians. Boston's founders set aside the Boston Common as pasture for grazing cows; today's urban activists are tending city farms and raising fresh fruit and vegetables in vacant lots and schoolyards, including schools all around Cambridge that host CitySprouts gardens, where children learn about science and history through tending (and eating!) vegetables, flowers, and other plants. Bostonians of yore tore down Mount Vernon, Beacon, and Pemberton Hills to make more land; today, Bostonians are digging out tunnels to make more hills at Danehy and Millennium Parks. Public-spirited citizens commissioned the grand Emerald Necklace parks to provide a respite for residents oppressed by the stresses of city life; today, public-spirited institutions are installing innovative green roofs and stormwater gardens at places like the Stata Center, the Children's Museum, and on the Harvard University campus, to protect our rivers and ocean from the stresses of city pollution. Boston's landscape is still growing and changing to answer the needs of its people and the environment.

Although much of Boston's public landscape was developed for practical purposes, there were other, deeper reasons why Bostonians built so many parks. Some of the nineteenth-century Bostonians who established

the Emerald Necklace and other grand parks were inspired by the spirit of Transcendentalism, a movement that began outside Boston in the 1830s. Transcendentalism's central tenet was that each person could find a transcendent spiritual connection to the divine, especially through direct experience with nature. Ralph Waldo Emerson, one of Transcendentalism's founders, wrote, "In the presence of nature, a wild delight runs through the man." Since every piece of forest within twenty miles of 1830s Boston was either farmland or a woodlot for harvesting timber and firewood, including the woods around Transcendentalist Henry David Thoreau's beloved Walden Pond, Bostonians had to seek this contact with nature by recreating nature—from scratch.

The underlying structure of Boston's landscape can be explained in one word: ice. From about seventy-five thousand to fifteen thousand years ago, the Laurentide Ice Sheet covered the northeastern United States from Maine to New Jersey and west to the Great Lakes. As the glaciers retreated, they scoured some places down to bedrock; in others, the glaciers deposited sand, rocks, or layers of till—a mix of rocks and sediment—either flat in the ground or into round asymmetrical hills called drumlins. Orient Heights in East Boston is a drumlin, as are most of the Boston Harbor Islands. Sometimes large chunks of glaciers calved and melted on-site, creating kettle lakes at many sites, including Jamaica Pond and Walden Pond. The glaciers also shifted large boulders to new locations. These massive rocks, known as "glacial erratics," can be seen in many of the wilder parks around the city, including Stony Brook Reservation and the Lynn Woods.

Boston lies in the Boston Basin, a low-lying area roughly bordered by Lynn to the north, Blue Hills Reservation to the south, and hills in Waltham and Newton to the west. When Europeans arrived nearly four hundred years ago, Boston was the Shawmut Peninsula, a hilly bulge shaped by glaciers and connected to the coast by a long, narrow neck of land. The settlers were drawn to the Shawmut by a fresh-water spring on what is now Beacon Hill; their original settlement in Charlestown had no ready source of good drinking water.

The first public open space in the city was the Boston Common, an open field established in 1634 for grazing cows, training militias, and holding large events, like public hangings. For more than one hundred and fifty years, the Common was the city's only public park while Bostonians went about their business of building homes and churches, sailing merchant ships, and starting the American Revolution.

The need for additional green space became apparent by the time the United States began electing presidents. At the turn of the nineteenth century, the Public Garden was a marsh, and the Back Bay really was the back bay of the Charles River, a tidal mud flat where residents could dig for clams—and where local sewage was dumped to wash out to sea. Alas, the Roxbury and Boston Mill Company built a dam across the Back Bay in 1821. The structure blocked the daily tides from washing away Boston's wastes, and both the Back Bay and the Public Garden sites became reeking, disease-ridden swamps. An 1849 report cited in Nancy Seasholes's book about Boston's man-made land, *Gaining Ground*, stated: "Back Bay at this hour is nothing less than a great cesspool, into which is daily deposited all the filth of a large and constantly increasing population. ... A greenish scum, many yards wide, stretches along the shores of the basin as far as the western Avenue [Mill Dam], whilst the surface of the water beyond is seen bubbling like a cauldron with the noxious gases that are exploding from the corrupting mass below." Boston was running out of land and clean water.

With Yankee ingenuity, Bostonians decided to solve the two problems at once: they would eliminate the fetid swamps by making more land. Bostonians had been filling in mud flats since they first arrived. They had carted away the tops of Beacon Hill and its erstwhile neighbors Pemberton Hill and Mount Vernon to make more dry ground but began to fill in the Back Bay in earnest in 1858. Over the next thirty years, four hundred acres were created and fifteen hundred homes were built, but poor water management led to another aromatic mess. Enter Frederick Law Olmsted and his vision for the Back Bay Fens as an ingenious solution to the poor water management—a park and detention basin rolled up into one lovely package. That approach to engineering natural spaces—answering the city's environmental and public health needs simultaneously—remains with us today.

Just prior to Olmsted, the approach earned a foothold in response to Boston's deceased residents' running out of space. Boston's burial grounds were so full that several corpses were laid in a single

grave, and some graves were left open until enough bodies could be found to fill them. In response, Bostonians established new suburban cemeteries that were designed as gardens as well as resting places, such as Forest Hills and Mount Auburn in Cambridge. These well-crafted landscapes were supposed to comfort grief and allow visitors to contemplate the glory of God's healing their loss through beauty—or at least give the deceased a little more elbow room.

Like Mount Auburn Cemetery's founders, Olmsted believed firmly in the curative power of landscape. Olmsted held that the only way to recover from the stresses of the built environment was to view a "natural" landscape that did not look obviously planted or designed. From 1878 to 1896, Frederick Law Olmsted designed most of what came to be known as the Emerald Necklace—from the Back Bay Fens to Franklin Park—to improve the environment and preserve public health. In the late nineteenth century, Boston's parks were seen as a necessary antidote to urban stresses, not just aids to spiritual development. Franklin Park, Olmsted's great escape for Bostonians, still shows traces of its rustic beginnings, and the curative power of landscape is as important today as it was then.

The early twentieth century was not kind to Boston's parks. Maintaining all the nineteenth-century parks took a great deal of money and attention. Very few new parks were established, although nonprofits preserved some estates with historic landscapes, including Roxbury's Shirley Eustis House and the Longfellow National Historic Site in Cambridge, as well as many large suburban estates. Worse, in the 1950s through the 1970s, many northeastern urban centers deteriorated, including Boston's. Wealthier residents moved to the suburbs, taking their political connections with them. Inner-city parks slid into

decay or even had parts of their grounds sold for parking lots. The 1980s and 1990s brought new money to Massachusetts parks, and many sites were revived, but some still bear scars of neglect.

In the last two decades, ingenious Bostonians have been working hard to make their city green again, finding (or creating) new places to build new parks. Beautiful new small parks have been created in unexpected areas—Ramler Park sits on a side street near Fenway Park, and a charming garden enlivens a courtyard at the Honan-Allston Branch Library. Some of Boston's most intriguing parks are actually green roofs: the Howard Ulfelder MD Healing Garden at Massachusetts General Hospital is located on an eighth-floor terrace with stunning views, while the park at Post Office Square conceals a seven-story underground parking garage.

Public works projects have been digging tunnels and then creating great mountains out of the fill at Deer and Spectacle Islands, Danehy Park, Cambridge, and Millennium Park in West Roxbury. The Rose Kennedy Greenway grows atop the Big Dig's tunnels for Route 93, bringing splashing fountains and butterflies to some of Boston's busiest streets. The Food Project has found places to farm on some of Boston's most crowded streets and on top of a parking garage, and the Boston Harborwalk has connected new green spaces to the sea.

Today's Bostonians are transforming their landscape with plants, earth, water, and sun. This book is your guide to over one hundred sites of interest in Boston's ever-expanding great green world.

It's time to get outside!

1. The Emerald Necklace

SWAN BOATS AND TULIPS, GREEN VISTAS AND FESTIVALS, GRAND boulevards with stately trees, and cool walks by quiet rivers—the Emerald Necklace of parks lets Bostonians rest and frolic in the heart of the city. This interconnected series of nine parks curls around Boston for seven miles, spanning eleven hundred acres and providing space for all manner of outdoor entertainment. Fly a kite on Boston Common's great lawns, promenade on the Commonwealth Avenue Mall, or stroll along the shady paths of the Back Bay Fens.

LEFT: JAMES P. KELLEHER ROSE GARDEN, THE FENS. ABOVE: BOSTON PUBLIC GARDEN.

Boston Common

Bounded by Tremont, Beacon, Charles, Park,
and Boylston Streets
617-357-8300
www.cityofboston.gov; Search: Boston Common
Open all year, 6:00AM–11:30PM
Handicap accessible
Free

Two hundred and forty years before Frederick Law Olmsted arrived in town, Boston's settlers bought about fifty acres of land from William Blaxton "for the common use of the inhabitants of Boston as a training field and cow pasture." Since 1634, the Boston Common, the nation's oldest public park, has lost its cows, sheep, and militia practices but maintained a long tradition of free speech and political activism.

Frederick Law Olmsted never touched the Boston Common, but his son did. In 1910 Frederick Law Olmsted Jr. began a three-year renovation that included replanting trees and putting in more soil. Today,

the Common is graced with over seven hundred trees—40 percent fewer than were growing there in 1850, but a respectable collection nonetheless. Almost two hundred of those trees are elms, which receive copious injections of fungicides every year to battle Dutch elm disease. None are as stately as the historic Great Elm, which supposedly stood on the Common from the arrival of the first European colonists until it was blown down in 1876. The tree is memorialized in a small plaque set in the ground in a grassy part of the park.

Before Olmsted Jr., the Common developed into a public park gradually. Its public life began as an open piece of scrubland not far from what was then the Charles River's tidal flat. The land was quickly overgrazed, in a classic example of the tragedy of the commons. Since no one paid for damage to the Common, everyone pastured as many cows as possible on the site, and the grass was ruined. However, in 1646, the men of Boston voted to limit grazing to seventy "milch cows." This new rule kept the Common a successful pasture for over one hundred years.

As time went on, more and more groups used the Common in different ways. Starting in 1660, Bostonians built a series of almshouses on the east side of the Common, near Park and Beacon Streets, to shelter the poor. In 1675, a formal walkway was laid out on the pasture. On the south side of the Common, along Tremont Street, Bostonians planted an allée of lime trees, elms, and poplars from 1723 to 1734 so that elegant citizens could promenade on a pleasant path. In 1830, cows were banned from the site.

Eventually, the Common's four hills were carried off to fill in land around the city, a regrade that left just one hill (Flagstaff Hill), and three ponds were reduced to a single pond (Frog Pond). Entrepreneurs used sites on the land to build warehouses, make

bricks, and even build a windmill. By the end of the nineteenth century, Bostonians were protecting their park from encroachment. In 1893, fifteen hundred Boston women turned out to protest a plan to lay trolley tracks across the park. The city ran the tracks underground instead, creating the nation's first subway. In the twentieth century, even cars moved underground: a three-story garage was built under the Common in 1962.

The history of gatherings and protests at the Common is varied. After the Revolution, the park was used for grand celebrations—honoring a visit by Revolutionary War hero Marquis de Lafayette in 1825, marking the first public water drawn into Boston from Natick's Lake Cochituate in 1848. In the twentieth century, upwards of one hundred thousand visitors at a time gathered to hear luminaries such as Charles Lindbergh, Martin Luther King Jr., Judy Garland, and Pope John Paul II. An equally large crowd came to protest the Vietnam War in 1969. Over two hundred permits for large assemblies are issued each year for group events as varied as yarn enthusiast "knit-outs," Shakespeare performances, and the Boston Freedom Rally for marijuana legalization.

Not all gatherings in the Common's history were peaceful. As one of the few large open public spaces of the Colonial period, the Common was the obvious space for the largest public gatherings: hangings. One famous victim was Mary Dyer, a Quaker missionary in Puritan Boston. Executed for her beliefs in 1660, Dyer is honored with a statue erected in 1959 at the State House, across Beacon Street from the Common. A food riot broke out on the Common in 1713. The American Sons of Liberty gathered at the Common for their protests in

1765–1766 and to tar and feather British officers. In 1768, over seventeen hundred and fifty British soldiers began an encampment on the Common and stayed there until they evacuated the city in 1776. The British ventured from their encampment on April 18, 1775, to travel to Lexington and Concord—and returned the next day from the first battles of the Revolutionary War. In 1835, an angry mob dragged abolitionist newspaper editor William Lloyd Garrison to the Common, broke his glasses, and tied a rope around his waist before he was rescued.

Today, the Boston Common is a lively urban center frequented by residents and visitors to the city. When there isn't a rally going on, visitors can enjoy strolling on the Common's leafy avenues to a seasonal skating rink and spray park, a playground with silly bronze frogs, a fountain, a bandstand, ball fields, and a large open lawn for sunbathing. History buffs can view several sculpted monuments to war heroes and the Central Burying Ground and the memorial relief at Beacon and Park Streets for Robert Gould Shaw, who died in 1863 while serving as colonel in command of the African American Fifty-fourth Massachusetts Volunteer Infantry in the Civil War.

Boston Public Garden

Bounded by Arlington, Beacon, Charles, and Boylston Streets
617-357-8300
www.cityofboston.gov; Search: Public Garden
Open all year, 6:00AM–11:30PM
Handicap accessible
Free

Frothy, flowery, with a lagoon full of swan boats and celebrity ducklings, the Public Garden is the antithesis to the great Common. This pretty little park covers twenty-five acres with graceful trees and Victorian-styled flower plantings. Come here to revel in floral artifice—radiant flower beds chock full of shocking pink roses, dazzling annual flowers, perky spring bulbs, and gaudy dark-chocolate cannas.

Like much of the Emerald Necklace, the Public Garden began as a sewage management project. The area was known as Round Marsh in Boston's early days, but by the 1820s, a dam cut the site off from the river. Without the daily tides washing the marsh clean, the site quickly became a stagnant swamp. In the early 1830s, the city covered the polluted flats with fill but left the area undeveloped.

Enter the horticulturists. In 1837, seventeen wealthy Bostonians headed by Horace Gray approached the city with a proposal to create a botanic garden and were granted access to the site. A combined aviary and conservatory was built, surrounded by pleasure grounds sporting the first tulips planted in America. Unfortunately, the conservatory burned down in 1847, and Gray's fortune collapsed as well. In 1852, the city reclaimed the land, and in 1860 George Meacham was commissioned to redesign the park.

Meacham's original plan survives to this day. Entering the garden from Arlington Street, visitors

first encounter Thomas Ball's 1869 statue of George Washington on his horse. From Washington, a straight path framed by formal flower beds rides through the center of the garden. The Boston Parks and Recreation Department fills the beds with hot-colored annuals each year in keeping with Victorian gardening sensibilities; if you like orange, you'll love the garden.

The path continues on a bridge over the park's central feature, a curving four acre lagoon inspired by the Serpentine in London's Hyde Park. The lagoon is where the Swan Boats swim—foot-powered flotillas inspired by the swan-powered boat in the opera *Lohengrin*. Real swans and plenty of ducks swim here too. The grassy shores are lined with weeping willows; their leaves appear pale yellow and ethereal when their neighboring weeping cherry trees burst with rosy blossoms in the spring.

Other paths wind through the garden's trees and sunny flower beds, eventually reaching monuments to Boston's departed citizens. The shady Boylston Street side features sculptured memorials to various prominent nineteenth century Bostonian Unitarian ministers, war heroes, and abolitionists. Around the corner at the Arlington Street entrance at Newbury Street is Boston's September 11 memorial, a low wall of pink granite etched with the names of Bostonians who died that awful day. The most unusual monument in the Public Garden lies to the north of George Washington near Arlington Street. There rests the 1866 Ether Monument, a tribute to the first successful use of anesthetic in surgery, in Boston in 1846. A tall column with lions' heads carved at its base is topped with a Good Samaritan comforting a child.

Children's joyful cries from the Beacon Street side of the park announce the *Make Way for Ducklings* statues. Generations of children who have read Robert McCloskey's book *Make Way for Ducklings* have come to the Public Garden to sit on the low backs of each of the bronze statues of that volume's famous birds: Jack, Kack, Lack, Mack, Nack, Ouack, Pack, and Quack, as well as Mrs. Mallard.

At its full glory in the 1860s, the Public Garden boasted four hundred tulip beds, twenty thousand roses, and six hundred trees representing thirty species. Today, there are a mere four rose beds, but the garden hosts eighty species of plants and flowers—many of them annuals nurtured in Boston city greenhouses—and, true to its botanical beginnings, one hundred and twenty-five species of trees. The most notable specimen trees are mapped on the Public Garden's website; they include a (small) giant redwood, a Kentucky coffee tree, a pagoda tree, and a Camperdown elm.

Commonwealth Avenue Mall

Commonwealth Avenue from Arlington Street to Kenmore Square, Boston
617-357-8300
www.cityofboston.gov; Search: Commonwealth Avenue Mall
Open all year, all day
Handicap accessible
Free

Boston's grandest boulevard, the Commonwealth Avenue Mall, is a spacious pedestrian promenade—a 100-foot-wide, 1.25-mile-long park with a broad walkway alongside some of Boston's most elegant nineteenth century buildings. Despite the nearby Commonwealth Avenue traffic, the mall walk is positively bucolic. It's flanked by wide lawns and shaded by a canopy of elms, sweet gums, green ashes, maples, lindens, and Japanese pagoda and zelkova trees.

When the state began to make new land by filling in the Back Bay tidal basin in 1858, Bostonians chose Arthur Gilman's plan for Commonwealth Avenue, a design for a boulevard like the great streets of Paris. (Modeling after France was very fashionable at the time; the Back Bay's mansard roofs are another symptom of the decade's Francophilia.) The Back Bay became a fashionable neighborhood almost immediately after the park was built.

The mall runs down the center of Commonwealth Avenue, linking the Public Garden with the Back Bay Fens. The simple linear design of a paved walkway under trees is lovely. In May, hundreds of magnolia trees bloom in front of Back Bay homes.

The center of the mall is populated by monuments to an assortment of honorees, including Alexander Hamilton, first Secretary of the U.S. Treasury, near Arlington Street; William Lloyd Garrison, editor and abolitionist, near Dartmouth Street; and Leif Eriksson, Viking explorer. Eriksson was placed

near Charlesgate East by Harvard professor Eben Horsford, who invented commercial manufacturing processes for baking powder and condensed milk, and a strange story tracing the Vikings to Weston, Massachusetts. Horsford funded the statue to honor Boston's scant Nordic past. The contributions of Phyllis Wheatley, Lucy Stone, and Abigail Adams are honored with statues at the 2003 Women's Memorial between Fairfield and Gloucester Streets. The most haunting sculpture on the mall is the Vendome Memorial, near Dartmouth Street: a low, black granite wall curves across the center of the walkway, a bronzed folded fireman's coat and helmet lie on top in commemoration of nine firefighters who died fighting a blaze at the nearby Vendome Hotel in 1972.

Like the Boston Common and the Public Garden, the Commonwealth Avenue Mall was built before Frederick Law Olmsted arrived in Boston. Olmsted's firm only designed the portion of the mall from Charlesgate East to Kenmore Square—and even that part was later rearranged by Arthur Shurcliff.

It is unexpected that Olmsted, designer of the Arnold Arboretum, tried to persuade the city to tear out most of the mall's trees. When asked in 1880 to advise the city on new tree plantings on the mall, Olmsted and his partner Charles Sprague Sargent replied that the city should tear out the existing trees and replace them with two lines of elms "to obtain ... the uniformity which seems to us essential to the future beauty and dignity of the finest street in the city." Whether from frugality or fear of public outcry, the city kept the existing mix of trees. Of course, there were some elms on the mall—most of which died of Dutch elm disease in twentieth century; ninety of them expired in 1968 alone. Eternal vigilance and annual fungicide injections are keeping the scourge at bay for now.

Back Bay Fens

Charlesgate/Boylston Street to Brookline Avenue, Boston
617-357-8300
www.cityofboston.gov; Search: Back Bay Fens
Open all year, all day
Handicap accessible
Free

The Back Bay Fens aren't nearly as famous as Fenway Park next door, where the Boston Red Sox battle the Yankees and other mighty foes. This lengthy, curving park follows the path of Boston's Muddy River from Brookline Avenue to the Charles River. Towering trees shading venerable stone bridges—landscapes designed by Frederick Law Olmsted—give much of the Fens a moody feel, a sense of a more ancient place far from the city's orderly streets and potted plants. Other parts of the Fens remade during and after Arthur Shurcliff's redesign are positively perky. The Kelleher Rose Garden, playing fields, a playground, and what is likely the largest community garden in Boston make the Fens a colorful, active park.

Like the Back Bay and the Public Garden, the Back Bay Fens were once tidal marshes (a "fen" is a marshy area), and much of Boston's sewage oozed onto its fetid plain. After an 1821 dam blocked the tides from reaching the Muddy River, the Fens area became what an engineer quoted in Nancy Seasholes's *Gaining Ground* called "the filthiest marsh and mud flats to be found anywhere in Massachusetts...a body of water so foul that

even clams and eels cannot live in it, and that no one will go within half a mile of in the summer unless from necessity, so great is the stench arising therefrom." The city contemplated building a giant granite block–lined detention pond on the site for stormwater from the Muddy River and Stony Brook.

Instead, Olmsted proposed a radical idea: to not just pipe the water through the land but to recreate the kind of natural system that would have filtered the water before the city was built. The Back Bay Fens became a giant water management project designed to look wild. From 1877 to 1894, Olmsted built an artificial marsh. Olmsted built gradually sloping banks around the river and created low islands planted with salt-tolerant cattails and other marsh plants. The landscaping was designed to evoke "the margins of salt creeks and harsh, weather-beaten headland."

Unfortunately, the Fens' natural filters were quickly dismantled. The drainage system failed repeatedly, and sewer breaks in 1897 and 1900 returned the Muddy River to its earlier condition and forced the city to build new underground conduits for sewage and the Stony Brook's flood overflows. The construction of the Charles River Dam in 1910 blocked any salt water from reaching the Charles—or the Fens—at all. With no need for a flood plain or salt-tolerant vegetation, Bostonians decided to get rid of all the marsh plants, put in grass at the edges of the Muddy River, and fill in acres of wetlands. The Roberto Clemente Field, the Fenway Victory Gardens, and the Kelleher Rose Gardens are all built on post-1900 fill. Altering the original landscape further, the 1960s-era construction of the Bowker Overpass and the Charlesgate entrance to Storrow Drive destroyed the Fens' connection to the Charles River and made it difficult for pedestrians to reach the Fens from the Commonwealth Avenue Mall. In

1954, Sears Roebuck even bought a few acres of the Fens and paved them over for a parking lot.

All this destruction of waterways took its toll. Disastrous floods in 1996 and 1998 caused over $100 million in property damage in the area. Since then, the city has undertaken a project to restore the Muddy River's flood capacity by dredging the river of sediment, removing invasive plants, and, most intriguingly, "daylighting" the river, bringing it back into the open air from its conduit at Landmark Center (Park Drive and Brookline Avenue).

What remains is not Olmsted's vision of "scenery of a winding, brackish creek, within wooded banks; gaining interest from the meandering course of the water," but a large, varied urban park as redesigned by Arthur Shurcliff in the 1920s. In many places, views of what is left of the river are blocked by huge stands of tall phragmites reeds, invasive non-native plants that infest much of the Emerald Necklace; they do lend a mysterious air to the banks near Agassiz Road and Park Drive though.

At the intersection of Park Drive and Boylston Street is the jumbled, glorious, near-infinite plot of the Fenway Victory Gardens (see chapter 10). Further south along Park Drive are memorials to World War II, Korean War, and Vietnam War dead and another Shurcliff addition, the James P. Kelleher Rose Garden.

The rose garden, named for the Boston city horticultural superintendent who revived the garden in the 1970s, is partly obscured by a yew hedge—but oh, what lies within! Two thousand roses, spanning over one hundred carefully labeled varieties, bloom and bloom and bloom from June through September. They jump up trellises, cascade from containers, billow onto paths, and curl up next to a small formal fountain. It's a fluffy, happy place, the weeping female nude statue and Japanese peace bell notwithstanding.

Cross over to the Fenway side near Forsyth Street if you wish to sojourn in quieter, darker woods by the Muddy River. In 2008, the Museum of Fine Arts across the street re-opened its Fenway-facing entrance for the first time in three decades, so you may find yourself with plenty of company.

Riverway

Parallels the Riverway from Park Drive to
Huntington Avenue, Boston
617-357-8300
www.cityofboston.gov; Search: Riverway
Open all year, all day
Handicap accessible
Free

The Riverway has no great monuments, no flower gardens, no catastrophic drainage problems—and no natural landscape. This narrow park is a twenty-five-acre river valley designed by Olmsted to look like a forest. Once bordered by quiet carriage roads, today's Riverway is flanked by a busy street and the MBTA Green Line trolleys—yet it is still a tranquil, lovely place.

In contrast to his other Emerald Necklace parks, Olmsted came up with the idea for the Riverway himself and offered it to the Boston park commissioners as an alternative to routing the Muddy River through an underground conduit.

The land itself was left pretty much alone on the Boston side of the park, which was already forested. On the Brookline side of the park, Olmsted had a berm built next to the railroad line to hide the engines from his park's visitors. Even today, the Green Line trolleys are invisible to passers-by. The land was filled and shaped, and the river was moved according to Olmsted's plan—even the boundary between Boston and Brookline was moved to ensure that it would stay in the middle of the river.

Similar to today, even late nineteenth-century naturalists battled over the inclusion of native or non-native plants in landscaped terrain. Olmsted certainly favored native plants, but he was primarily interested in producing a certain type of visual landscape and happily used non-natives to create a varied environment. By contrast Professor Charles Sprague Sargent, first director of the Arnold Arboretum and a leader of Brookline's park commissioners, was a native plant chauvinist. Sprague fought with Olmsted over whether species that originated outside New England belonged along the Muddy River. Record shows he crossed out Olmsted's planting lists and generally made a fuss. Astute observers in the park today can find evidence of their quarrels. The Brookline side is mostly northern red and white oaks; the Olmsted-controlled Boston side

of the park may still have some sweet gum trees, magnolias, and oaks that are uncommon in New England, including bur oak and swamp white oak.

Walking along the Riverway will take you past towering oaks and slender birches, stone bridges, and the Round House, a rustic stone shelter with a squat conical roof. One bridge arches over a bridle path that disappeared long ago.

Olmsted Park

Bounded by Pond Avenue/Jamaicaway and Perkins Street, Brookline/Jamaica Plain
617-357-8300
www.cityofboston.gov; Search: Olmsted
Open all year, all day
Handicap accessible
Free

Mrs. Mallard of *Make Way for Ducklings* would have had access to much more ducky real estate if she'd decided to move to Olmsted Park instead of the Public Garden. Olmsted designed his namesake

park to be "a chain of picturesque fresh-water ponds, alternating with attractive natural groves and meads." A duck could choose from three large ponds—Leverett Pond, Willow Pond, and Ward's Pond—and still find seventeen acres of forest to shade her nest. Ducks and humans alike can gaze across the water into the trees and contemplate life, or at least where to find more bread crumbs.

Part of the grand Muddy River improvement project extending to the Back Bay Fens, Olmsted Park is another example of Olmsted's water works. Olmsted excavated Leverett Pond (now at Pond Avenue and Leverett Street) not only to create a detention pond for Muddy River floodwaters but also to beautify the landscape. To that end, Olmsted had the Brookline Town Brook diverted through conduits to make sure there was enough water to fill the pond. Olmsted had also planned for a series of "natural history pools" for a zoo between Willow Pond and Ward's Pond (approximately Willow Pond Road and Perkins Street). Unfortunately, the Boston Society of Natural History never raised enough money to build it, and in 1899 the ponds were filled in.

Unlike the sculpted valleys and banks at Riverway and the Back Bay Fens, constructed to appear natural, the higher ground in Olmsted Park is mostly untouched. Glacial scrapings and meanderings shaped the terrain long ago. Ward's Pond (near Perkins Street) is a glacial kettle pond formed when a retreating glacier split and left its remains to melt into Brookline's earth over twelve thousand years ago. The greatest change humans ever wrought was the flattening of an Olmsted-planned meadow by Leverett Pond into a baseball diamond (Daisy Field).

Apart from the playing field, Olmsted Park consists of open oak woods. While ducks will prefer to travel via Muddy River streams, humans can walk on shady paths, six stone bridges, and a boardwalk around Ward's Pond. Other bipedal visitors can enjoy separate bicycle and walking paths along Pond Avenue between Chestnut Street and Willow Pond Road.

Jamaica Pond

Jamaicaway by Pond Street/Parkman Drive,
Jamaica Plain
617-357-8300
www.cityofboston.gov; Search: Jamaica Pond
Open all year, all day; Boat House open
9:00AM–6:00PM daily, April–October
Handicap accessible
Free

The Muddy River it's not. Jamaica Pond, one-time drinking water source for part of Boston, is a grand sixty acres of water so naturally attractive that Olmsted barely touched the ground before declaring it a park. He described the place in 1876 as "a natural sheet of water, with quiet, graceful shores … for the most part shaded by a fine natural forest-growth." Today, the traffic and creeping development nearby don't feel terribly natural, but the narrow park around the pond itself features paved walking paths under swaying trees, a nature center, and an unparalleled sense of space and distance in an old, crowded city.

Like nearby Ward's Pond, Jamaica Pond is a glacial kettle pond. It was created when the retreating Laurentide glacial ice calved a gigantic lump of ice over twelve thousand years ago. Given that the ice formed a ninety-foot-deep, sixty-acre pond, you can imagine how large it was *before* it melted.

Jamaica Pond is the largest body of fresh water near Boston, and it was an important water source for part of the city in the nineteenth century. After

Boston began drawing water from Lake Cochituate in 1848, Jamaica Pond quickly became a center for ice-harvesting instead. In the days before refrigeration, ice was cut from ponds in the winter and stored in insulated houses, then delivered to customers in the warmer months to cool their iceboxes. Boston's ice was shipped as far away as Rio de Janeiro and Calcutta. At its 1880 peak, the Jamaica Pond Ice Company had twenty-two ice houses on Jamaica Pond and could store up to thirty thousand tons of ice. Unfortunately, the company used hundreds of horses to haul all this ice, and their manure polluted the pond.

The pond was also a popular place for sailing and skating during the nineteenth century. By the time Jamaica Park was planned in 1890, Boston's wealthier residents had been building summer homes by the pond for almost a century. Unfortunately, these tasteful neighbors had bid up the value of local real estate so much that Boston's park commissioners could only afford to purchase sixty acres of land. That acquisition left only a narrow shoreline around much of the pond.

Olmsted had almost all the ice houses and summer homes removed. However, Olmsted did not touch Pinebank, the Francis Parkman house—the only pre-existing building that remained in the Emerald Necklace for over one hundred years. Olmsted no doubt admired Pinebank's site overlooking the north side of the pond from a high bluff. After years of fire and neglect though, Pinebank was condemned and removed by the city of Boston in 2007; its name lives on in Pinebank Promontory.

Today, Jamaica Pond includes eleven acres covered by trees, many of which frame and shade the 1.4-mile-long paved path around the pond. Some groves of pines, oaks, and copper beeches survive from Olmsted's plantings, and the park is sprinkled with hawthorns, cherries, and dogwoods

planted in the early twentieth century. All manner of water birds cool their legs in Jamaica's welcoming waters. If the plants are too still and the birds too flighty for fishermen, they'll be pleased with the state's stocking the pond, which hosts rainbow, brown, and tiger trout, bluegill, large mouth bass, yellow perch, hornpout catfish, pickerel, and sunfish. Don't bring your bicycle—the 1.4-mile path around the pond is strictly limited to foot traffic. Disobey, and fear the ire of the Boston Park Ranger Nature Center (Jamaicaway at Pond Street) staff, who patrol the pond when they're not leading public nature programs.

If you want to go faster than your feet can carry you, your best bet during summer months is to rent a boat. Don't fall in though; only waterfowl are allowed to swim in this pond.

Arnold Arboretum

125 Arborway, Boston
617-524-1718 | arboretum.harvard.edu
Arboretum grounds open year-round, dawn to dusk. Visitor Center (Hunnewell Building) open 9:00AM–4:00PM, Monday–Friday; 10:00AM–4:00PM, Saturday; noon–4:00PM, Sunday; closed holidays
Handicap accessible
Free

It's easy to figure out where to start exploring the Arnold Arboretum: the Hunnewell Building at the Arborway entrance, which houses the sole public bathroom in the arboretum. But where can you stop exploring? The arboretum has two hundred and sixty-five acres of forests, meadows, wetlands, and ponds with forty-five hundred varieties of woody plants and fifteen thousand trees. Put on your walking shoes and pump up your bicycle tires: cars are not permitted in the Arnold Arboretum, and you're going to have to go a long way to explore it all. (Visitors with special needs may reserve vehicle permits in advance.)

The Arnold Arboretum is named for James Arnold, a wealthy New Bedford merchant who had helped found the New Bedford Horticultural Society. When Arnold died in 1868, his will directed that his estate be used "for the promotion of Agricultural or Horticultural improvements." One of his trustees, educator and tree expert George B. Emerson, suggested that the money go toward creating an arboretum—literally a museum of trees. The funds were given over to Harvard University, which already maintained a seven-acre botanic garden in Cambridge on the aptly named Garden Street. That space was far too small for collecting trees, and in 1872 Harvard's trustees agreed to use the Arnold money to create a new arboretum on the 210-acre Bussey Farm in Jamaica Plain. According to Arnold's will, that arboretum would contain "all the trees, shrubs, and herbaceous plants, either indigenous or exotic, which can be raised in the open air."

Arnold's bequest was large enough to purchase plenty of trees, but too small to fund anything else—like roads, buildings, or fences. In 1874, Charles Sprague Sargent, the arboretum's first director, wrote to Frederick Law Olmsted for help. Sargent proposed that the arboretum's land be given to the city, on condition that Sargent control the plantings "in order that the scientific objects of the trust could be carried out." Olmsted agreed to plan the park for the city, and the arboretum began to take shape. In 1882, the city of Boston purchased the land, and Harvard University signed a one-thousand-year lease for the park.

Olmsted and Sargent collaborated on the arboretum's layout—an immensely important job, as

the purpose of the arboretum was both to educate the public about trees and to provide a beautiful landscape. Together, they arranged the specimen trees in order by then-current ideas of family and genus and incorporated the site's existing woods into the design. After the arboretum's roads were in place, Sargent spent the rest of his life developing and overseeing the arboretum and traveling to South America, Europe, China, Taiwan, Japan, and Korea to collect as many woody plants as could be "raised in the open air" as possible. All told, the arboretum staff have introduced almost two thousand plants to the United States. The arboretum continues research programs in China and Thailand today.

Today, the arboretum's trees still stand in the same precise order, making walking tours a fascinating journey through strikingly different environments. Simply listing the genera represented is exhausting— maples, beeches, hickories, forsythia, honeysuckles, magnolias, oaks, rhododendrons. Amateur and expert arborists alike will be delighted. The arboretum carefully labels each plant with a distinctive tag bearing the plant's scientific name, common name, and where it was collected or grown. The arboretum's website is especially helpful for plant enthusiasts and features detailed maps of the locations of different species, lists of what flowers are in bloom each month, and a complete searchable inventory of the arboretum's collection of living plants. (Over five million specimens of dead plants and seeds display at the Harvard University Herbaria.)

All of these groups are planted In clumps, allowing analytical visitors to compare and contrast the specimens and allowing passionate visitors to revel in the sheer number and size of them. Stick to the broad paved paths or make your way through the woods. Groves of spreading lindens invite visitors to wander in their shady bowers, while upright spruces guard a steep hillside. Springtime visitors relish the sunny Bradley Rosaceous Collection, where cherries, apples, quinces, and yes, roses display their similarly shaped blooms. Other wanderers can explore the dark shaded reaches of Hemlock Hill.

Stroll up Peter's Hill for a charming view of Boston: the gold State House dome shines in the distance. It's an easier walk to the Larz Anderson Bonsai Collection, located in a single small house a quarter mile from the entrance. Adjoining the bonsai collection is the hillside M. Victor and Frances Leventritt Garden, a display of shrubs and vines which won a 2007 General Design Award of Excellence from the American Society of Landscape Architects for its striking terraced design.

The arboretum's mission is research, horticulture, and education, not simply providing park space, and some normal park activities are not allowed: picking flowers and eating. Picnicking is allowed on the grounds on just one day a year: Lilac Sunday, the arboretum's Mother's Day celebration, when upwards of fifty thousand people stroll through fragrant avenues formed by over four hundred lilacs (or sit on the ground and munch). If you visit at any other time, be prepared to feast your eyes but not your stomach.

Franklin Park

Bounded by Seaver Street/Blue Hill Avenue/
American Legion Highway/Morton Street, Boston
617-357-8300
www.cityofboston.gov; Search: Franklin Park
Open all year, all day
Handicap accessible
Free

Frederick Law Olmsted was so concerned that Franklin Park might be misunderstood that he published an entire book explaining its design: *Notes on the Plan of Franklin Park and Related Matters*. The park was intended to allow city dwellers to gaze on natural beauty and renew their minds and bodies with the glories of the green world. A century later, Franklin Park is still beautiful, but it has come to serve many purposes. It is the crown jewel of the Emerald Necklace: a 527-acre landscape with a grassy common, a garden, a mall, a former tidal marsh, a river glen, several ponds, and an arboretum and complex including a golf course, playgrounds, ball fields, a stadium, ruins, trails, a hospital, parking lots, ponds, streams, and—at the time of publication—a zoo.

A grand masterpiece of a park design, rivaled only by Olmsted's Central Park and Prospect Park in New York City, Franklin Park is a country park in the middle of a city. At one time, Franklin Park really was in the country. When Boston's park commissioners first proposed a park on the site in the 1870s, building in the area was sparse. The entire property only had a dozen small farms and some wooded hills. However, two railway lines passed the park, and Blue Hill Avenue had been built on the east side—an easy trip for city dwellers.

That access was the key to Olmsted's vision of the park. Like many of his cohorts, Olmsted thought of parks not only as a pleasant place to idle away an afternoon but also as the key to urban public health. Human minds and bodies damaged by the stress of city life could be restored by the experience of natural beauty. In his *Notes on the Plan of Franklin Park and Related Matters,* Olmsted wrote, "The chief end of a large park is an effect on the human organism by an action of what it presents to view, which action, like that of music, is of a kind that goes back of thought, and cannot be fully given the form of words."

Although the site was opened to the public in 1883, Olmsted actually designed Franklin Park from 1884 to 1885 on this "gentle valley nearly a mile in length." A nationwide financial depression and Boston's political struggles delayed work on the park. The park was named for Benjamin Franklin in attempt to use the funds from his estate to pay for the park, but it was to no avail; Franklin's heirs brought a lawsuit when the estate matured in 1891 and tied up the money for years. In the end, the

city used other money for the park, but Franklin's name stuck.

Olmsted conceived Franklin Park as a very simple design. He had written in 1870 that, instead of carefully coiffed gardens or architectural monuments, city parks should display "the beauty of the fields, the meadow, the prairie, of the green pastures, and the still waters. What we want to gain is tranquility and rest to the mind." Instead of framing a waterway or an educational tree display, Franklin Park was designed to highlight "a lovely dale gently winding between low wooded slopes, giving a broad expanse of unbroken turn, lost in the distance under scattered trees." Olmsted eschewed fancy plantings and grand earthworks for Franklin Park. Instead, he arranged flights of trees and built rustic stone shelters and arches.

The park was planned as two separate sections ringed by carriage roads, bridle paths, and walking trails: a country park, to be used for quiet contemplation and walks, and a much smaller ante-park, along Seaver Street, for sports and active recreation. The country park featured a broad lawn surrounded by more secluded spaces—a forested wilderness and the wooded slopes of Schoolmaster, Scarboro, and Hagborne Hills. Olmsted was adamant that the country park was supposed to serve as a place for natural scenery, a place to restore weary city dwellers' mental health with soothing sights—to the extent that the central meadow was supposed to be trimmed not by lawnmowers but sheep. All the more vigorous activities were appropriated to the ante-park, which was planned to include a "playstead" of fields for sports, a playground, a small naturalistic zoo of native animals, an amphitheater for concerts, and the "greeting," a half-mile mall for carriages and promenading pedestrians.

Olmsted's therapeutic division did not last long. All manner of large groups wanted to gather on the country park's lawn, and a golf course was set up in the country park's meadow in 1890. In 1892, Olmsted persuaded the city to acquire another forty-six acres nearby for gatherings and active sports at what is now Harambee Park, but Franklin Park was too tempting a site for the city to leave alone.

Since Olmsted published his final revised plan for the park in 1891, Franklin Park has acquired many facilities that Olmsted considered entirely inappropriate to a country park. From the 1920s onward Boston's park commissioners started building more amusements in the park to attract more visitors. While there is still plenty of restorative scenery in the park, visitors will also find a stadium and an eighteen-hole public golf course. The zoo was redesigned by Arthur Shurcliff in 1912 to accommodate more exotic animals in cages. In 1954, the Lemuel Shattuck Hospital was built on what was once the Heathfield section of the park, intended to evoke an abandoned pasture covered with flowers and vines. The greeting promenade was devoured by a Franklin Park Zoo expansion in 1978. Many of Olmsted's rustic stone shelters were removed by a parks superintendent in the early 1900s.

Today, visiting different sections of the park produces markedly different experiences. Many prominent features have no labels or signs, adding an air of mystery and a tinge of frustration. The most popular walk around the park is a 2.5-mile paved path simply called the Loop. A popular location for cross-country races, the Loop follows Circuit Drive from the Ellicott Arch to the Golf Club House then circles back past Scarborough Pond and Ellicott Dale. Travelers on the Loop get a sense of Olmsted's vision as they pass by wide vistas of the golf course's pleasant rolling hills, with trees in the distance. Start your walk at the Club House to take advantage of the only public restroom in the park.

Scarborough Pond, off the Loop near Shattuck Hospital, offers quiet views of red maples, ducks, and a stone bridge. Neighboring Scarborough Hill boasts groves of beech trees and more views of the golf course. Olmsted had planned a dairy here, with cows to munch on park grass and provide healthful milk for children, but it was never built.

Schoolmaster Hill, along the Loop near the center of the park, was once inhabited by Transcendentalist philosopher Ralph Waldo Emerson. It bears one of the few maps in the park—on a low rock by the road—and provides still more stone ruins to explore and views of the 116-acre public golf course that was once the country park's meadow. The lawn is now populated by flocks of Canada geese instead of sheep.

The sixty-five-acre wilderness area along Forest Hills Street is an oak forest with winding unmarked trails. On a walk there, visitors can find pleasant paths through open woods, groves of hemlocks and hickories, labeled specimen trees, or tangled confusing pathways next to thickets of invasive catbrier and Japanese knotweed. Great lumpy puddingstone boulders left by passing glaciers sit on high open slopes. Near Pierpont Road, the woods are full of stone ruins that give the place an air of an abandoned medieval castle site—overgrown steps and bridle paths and the remains of the Overlook Shelter. That shelter, the only building Olmsted ever designed, overlooked the playstead. It burned down in 1945; tall stone columns and low walls are all that remain.

Many people use Franklin Park for many different ends. There are festivals and races, plays and concerts; occasionally, there are also some urban annoyances, like motorbikes racing through the park on summer evenings and odd garbage dumped in the more remote areas. Franklin Park is not always the quiet, healing landscape that Olmsted had planned. Instead, it's an active part of an active city—yet easy to enjoy.

The Necklace's Designer: Frederick Law Olmsted

Born in Hartford, Connecticut, in 1822, Frederick Law Olmsted never had any formal training in landscape design, and he never attended college due to illness. Still, Olmsted's intelligence, enthusiasm, and his talents for administration and making social connections carried him through many trades before he found his calling as a landscape architect.

Olmsted's varied career included sailing as a merchant seaman, farming a tract on Long Island, and journalism. During the 1850s, he toured the South and Texas as a newspaper correspondent and published three much-quoted books and dozens of newspaper columns on his first-hand observations of slavery and local life. He became editor of *Putnam's Monthly Magazine* in 1855 and expected to spend his life editing—until the firm failed in 1857. Jobless, Olmsted applied for the position of superintendent of construction of New York's unbuilt Central Park. He got the job and then won Central Park's design competition in collaboration with trained architect Calvert Vaux. Olmsted worked with Vaux on several more parks before they parted ways in 1872.

Olmsted designed most of the Emerald Necklace's parks from 1878 to 1896. He created the Emerald Necklace not only for Bostonians' pleasure and exercise but also for their health. In the case of the Back Bay Fens, Olmsted had an immediate effect on Bostonians' physical health as he transformed Boston's Muddy River from a stagnant, fetid, sewage-filled mess into the most beautiful drainage project in New England. Still, Olmsted was even more concerned about the effect of parks on the human mind.

Like Charles Eliot and many other reformers of the time, Olmsted believed that people who lived in the city needed to have contact with nature, and not just any potted plant would do. In his 1886 *Notes on the Plan of Franklin Park and Related Matters*, Olmsted wrote, "A man's eyes cannot be as much occupied as they are in large cities by artificial things, or by natural things seen under obviously artificial conditions, without a harmful effect, first on his mental and nervous system and ultimately on his entire constitutional organization." For Olmsted, parks had to appear "natural," as though the land had been left to itself, even though Olmsted's Boston parks generally required moving tons of earth and replanting the entire landscape.

Additionally, the parks needed to be accessible to all residents, not just wealthy citizens who could visit rural estates in carriages. Olmsted's city landscapes were designed to bring the country to any city dweller that could walk. Today, modern Bostonians can still visit Olmsted's idealized landscapes and relax in his healing vision of green.

HEADING TO THE "BITTERSWEET CD" GEOCACHE IN ACTON.

THE "BITTERSWEET CD" GEOCACHE LOCATED AT N 42° 28.941 W 071° 29.111.

PHOTOS COURTESY MARGOT ANNE KELLEY, AUTHOR OF *LOCAL TREASURES: GEOCACHING ACROSS AMERICA.*

Letterboxing, Geocaching, and EarthCaching

If you see someone peering into the bushes while holding a beautifully bound notebook, watch carefully; that person might be on the verge of finding a letterbox. Waterproof boxes tucked away in dozens of parks around Boston hold special stamps, often handmade. Stamping your notebook is your reward for working through the puzzles that dozens of scheming stamp makers have left online at letterboxing.org.

The letterboxes and their clues have been assembled by hundreds of volunteers with an interest in treasure hunts. Boston proper has plenty of letterboxes with titles like "Max's Pondside Declaration" and "Twelve Spotted Dragonfly." Some instructions are simple, some are downright cryptic, but all of them are open for anyone to read and discover.

Geocaching enthusiasts also find surprises from clues on a website—but they use Global Positioning System (GPS) units to locate their treasures. Descriptions at geocaching.com include GPS coordinates and some hints at the location. However, the GPS coordinates are only available to visitors who have registered with the website, which is run by a private firm.

EarthCaching is a variant of geocaching. Instead of peeking into treasure boxes, EarthCachers use GPS coordinates to seek out geological features in the landscape: fault lines, signs of glaciers, dinosaur footprints. The sites are approved by the Geological Society of America at earthcache.org but administered by the geocaching folks.

Puddingstone

The most distinctive rocks around Boston are made of Roxbury puddingstone. Named for steamed puddings filled with dried fruit, this lumpy, bumpy conglomerate rock abounds in parks to the south of downtown in Jamaica Plain and Roxbury, including Franklin Park. As of 1983, Roxbury puddingstone became the state rock of Massachusetts.

2.   The Harborwalk:
   Boston's Sapphire Necklace

BOSTON'S MOST STUNNING PARKS LIE AT THE SPACE BETWEEN
land and sea. Over thirty-six miles of trails, parks, plazas, and viewpoints
stretch from East Boston to Dorchester. Traveling from north to south, the
Harborwalk's visitors can traipse along a six-hundred-foot promenade on the
water at Piers Park, splash in the fountain and smell the roses at Christopher
Columbus Waterfront Park, visit a Civil War fort on Castle Island, fly kites
over John Paul II Park's wide-open spaces, or explore verdant saltwater
marshes at Neponset Park—all within sight of salt water.

OPPOSITE: CHRISTOPHER COLUMBUS WATERFRONT PARK. ABOVE: CASTLE ISLAND.

Piers Park

95 Marginal Street, East Boston
617-428-2800
www.bostonharborwalk.com; Search: Piers Park
Open all year, dawn to dusk
Handicap accessible
Free

With a six-hundred-foot promenade over the inner harbor and a ravishing view of downtown Boston, Piers Park is one of the Harborwalk's most scenic spots. Built in 1995–1997 atop actual abandoned piers, Piers Park is where a city meets the sea, and where East Boston's dense neighborhoods and industrial sites give way to the water. Small sailboats flit about the park's dock courtesy of the Piers Park Sailing Center, a nonprofit which offers free sailing lessons to local youth. The park itself is a sea of green: six acres of grass, trees, flower beds, playgrounds, a sprinkle park, and an amphitheater, with curving brick walkways and Victorian-style street lamps to light your way at night.

In the late 1960s, the Massachusetts Port Authority (Massport) razed East Boston's Wood Island Park, a forty-six-acre park designed by Frederick Law Olmsted, to make room for another Logan Airport runway. (Some of the elms Olmsted planted still survive on Neptune Road next to the Wood Island T stop.) Local residents began to look for a new space that crowded East Boston could use for a park, and they came up with the idea of using abandoned piers. It took fifteen years for residents to convince Massport, the entity that runs nearby Logan Airport, to build Piers Park—but once Massport decided to build the park, it spent $17 million making it beautiful. Massport still maintains the park and provides security for this urban green space.

The park's most striking feature is the promenade. The walk begins at a brick plaza with four flagpoles looking like ships' masts sprouting out of the pier. Trees line the walkway here, and suspended wing-like shade structures protect benches from the sun. The promenade quickly takes visitors to two pavilions. The first pavilion, a square with sides facing the four cardinal directions, features twenty ornamental columns carved by sculptor William P. Reimann. The columns' designs depict symbols representing the fifty most populous ethnic identities in East Boston, as detailed in the 1990 census: owls, dragons, knots, trees, and dozens of other intricate glyphs face the waves.

The second pavilion is dedicated to East Boston's most famous ship builder, Donald McKay, whose *Flying Cloud* was one of the fastest clipper ships of all time. McKay's pavilion is a squat modernist

lighthouse with a conical roof. A spiral ramp leads visitors to the center light.

Unfortunately, the lovely westward views end at the park's iron fences, which border rotting abandoned piers. There are plans to develop Phase 2 of the park on the neighboring pier to the west, but so far the only green space there is provided by weeds.

Christopher Columbus Waterfront Park

Atlantic Avenue and Richmond Street, Boston
617-635-4505
www.bostonharborwalk.com; Search:
Christopher Columbus Waterfront Park
Open all year, dawn to dusk
Handicap accessible
Free

It's hard to believe that Christopher Columbus Waterfront Park is real. It's just too perfect. Plunked down on Boston's waterfront between the North End and Faneuil Hall, the 4.5-acre site stretches along the harbor. You can take a ride on a ferry at nearby Long Wharf or simply watch boats go by from any point. The wide paved walk along the

CHRISTOPHER COLUMBUS WATERFRONT PARK.

harbor's edge is a popular spot for festivals and evening concerts.

If the harbor views aren't sufficient entertainment, play Frisbee on the broad lawn, cavort on the spiffy gated playground, or splash in the harborside sprinkle park. Visitors with quieter dispositions can stroll under the 340-foot-long arched wisteria arbor or admire the small but lovely rose garden on the city side of the park. If you like your green space with gigabytes, bring your laptop and take advantage of the park's free wireless internet connection.

Castle Island

Day Boulevard, South Boston
617-727-5290
www.mass.gov/dcr; Search: Castle Island
Open all year, dawn to dusk
Handicap accessible
Free

An historic fort, a beach, kites, hot dogs, ships sailing out to sea—Castle Island is a sunny spot for families to play. Children romp through the elaborate playground and plead for hot dogs from Sullivan's, conveniently located at the park's entrance.

Castle Island really was an island in 1630. Since then, Bostonians have filled in so much of the harbor

BOTH PAGES: CASTLE ISLAND.

that the island is merely South Boston's eastern tip. Visitors can walk southwest from Castle Island to Carson Beach and beyond to UMass–Boston. (See chapter 7, "Green Art," for information on UMass's Arts on the Point.)

The twenty-two-acre park's most distinctive feature is Fort Independence, a pentagonal fort built of granite blocks from 1834 to 1851. Summer visitors are greeted by a costumed guide who wears a replica Civil War uniform—not a tricorne hat and knee breeches like at most other Boston sights.

Castle Island's charm is that it is an urban park actively used by Bostonians young and old and their dogs, who will happily stop and sniff children who greet them. You never forget you're in the city here. The eastern shore of this city park offers a fine view of the airport—and plenty of jet take-off rumblings to go with the view; the western shore's vista consists of large ship loading cranes. But no matter where you look, you are surrounded by the sparkling water of Boston Harbor. The greenery consists of grass and scattered stalwart trees. Although a healthy meadow is growing on Fort Independence's roof, seekers of a quiet, verdant oasis should look elsewhere.

POPE JOHN PAUL II PARK.

Pope John Paul II Park

Gallivan Boulevard/Hallet Street, Dorchester
617-727-6034
www.mass.gov/dcr; Search: Pope John Paul II Park
Open all year, dawn to dusk
Handicap accessible
Free

Wide-open and windy, Pope John Paul II Park's unshaded vistas show wetlands meadows, paths for walking and biking, a soccer field, a playground, and dozens of people enjoying the rolling green lawns. This sixty-five-acre park has been popular since it opened in 2001, giving densely developed Dorchester a welcome green oasis along the Neponset River.

The Neponset River has been an industrial site since Israel Stoughton built a grain mill on its shores in 1635. When the Metropolitan District Commission bought the land for Pope John Paul II Park in the 1970s, the park site was being used as a landfill, a drive-in movie theater, and a lumber yard. The landfill site had to be capped with several feet of clay and soil to keep pollution from the landfill from leaching into the river; trees could not be planted in much of the park for fear that the roots would break through the cap and release contaminants. Luckily, the soccer field and playground are located in the relatively uncontaminated drive-in site.

The park's salt marshes attract black ducks, mergansers, teal, snowy egrets, and great blue herons—but it's the luxury of open plains that attract visitors. The yearly East Meets West Kite and Cultural Festival takes full advantage of the site's breezy, treeless plains—in 2007, participants boosted a writhing three-hundred-foot-long dragon into the air. Bring a kite and binoculars and enjoy the view, or ride your bike and enjoy the three-mile Neponset River Greenway (chapter 14).

Neponset Park

Granite Avenue, Dorchester
617-727-6034
www.bostonharborwalk.com; Search:
Neponset Park
Open all year, dawn to dusk
Handicap accessible
Free

Like John Paul II Park, Neponset Park was developed on degraded land. The Neponset Park is a former auto body shop and scrap metal site, and the site's considerable rehabilitation included removing metals and auto wastes from the soil. Today, it's simply another lovely stop on the Neponset River Greenway.

John Paul II Park's next-door neighbor, the Neponset Park brings visitors to the water's edge—and into the Neponset River. This seven-acre park's most prominent feature is the boating ramp near the parking lot. Paddlers can launch canoes and kayaks and explore the nearby marshes. Children who would rather just get wet can enjoy a simple spray fountain. In cooler weather, people of all ages can stroll on the simple labyrinth outlined in the fountain's pavement and enjoy compact plantings of native trees and shrubs, as well as an open lawn and walkway.

Save the Harbor/Save the Bay

Want to see seals and porpoises in Boston Harbor? Or sail on the harbor's salty waves? Perhaps you'd just like to dabble your toes in the water at a clean beach. Save the Harbor/Save the Bay has worked for almost a quarter century to make the Boston Harbor clean and open to everyone.

The group was founded in 1986 by an attorney who'd begun a successful lawsuit to clean up Boston Harbor, the judge who heard the case, a reporter who covered the story for the Boston Globe, and a local mother who wanted her children to be able to swim in clean water. Since then, Save the Harbor/Save the Bay has worked tirelessly to ensure that Boston Harbor's water is safe for swimming, boating, and fishing.

Today, Save the Harbor/Save the Bay connects Boston communities to the sea through initiatives such as leading public-private coalitions to deal with water pollution and giving local groups seed money to hold sand castle contests—all while helping over four thousand children a year experience the harbor through day trips, camps, and Marine Mammal Safaris.

To help the harbor become even more beautiful, and to find those sand castle contests, check out the group's website at www.savetheharbor.org.

3. Fresh Water Green

WHEN THE HARBORWALK'S SEASIDE SUN IS TOO BRIGHT, RETIRE to Boston's cooler, greener fresh-water parks. Scoured out by retreating glaciers fifteen thousand years ago, Cambridge's Fresh Pond attracts strollers and migrating birds, and Walden Pond's history, shady trails, and swimming beach draw half a million visitors a year. If you'd rather relax by a river, the ever-popular Charles River Esplanade draws sunbathers, public concert goers, boaters, and other recreationists.

BOTH PAGES: CHARLES RIVER ESPLANADE.

Fresh Pond Reservation

Bounded by Fresh Pond Parkway, Concord
Avenue, Blanchard Avenue, Grove Street, and
Huron Avenue, Cambridge
617-349-4762 | www.cambridgema.gov;
Search: Fresh Pond | friendsoffreshpond.org
Open all year, dawn to dusk
Handicap accessible
Free

Fresh Pond really is fresh. The 155-acre Fresh
Pond Reservoir stores most of Cambridge's drinking
water received from outlying reservoirs. The pond
itself is fenced in to protect water quality—local
residents don't particularly want you dipping your
toes in their teacups—but the 162 acres surrounding
the pond are popular with walkers, joggers, bicyclists, and dogs, who have a separate swimming
beach on a neighboring pond all to their shaggy
selves. A shady paved path runs two-and-a quarter
miles around the pond, and trails lead into pockets
of woodlands. Fresh Pond has undergone a major
environmental restoration over the past decade.
Apart from the sparkling joys of brilliant water and
open sky, interested visitors can find a showcase of
ecological landscaping techniques along the pond's
shores, including stabilized forest slopes, a stormwater treatment wetland, and a butterfly meadow.

Like Jamaica Pond (chapter 1) and Walden Pond, Fresh Pond is a glacial kettle, formed when a chunk of the retreating Laurentide glacial cover broke off and melted in place fifteen thousand years ago. In Colonial times, the area reaching north from Fresh Pond toward Alewife Station and beyond was known as the Great Swamp, a vast, marshy wetland. Native Americans had seasonal fishing camps in the area, and four-thousand-year-old fishing weirs have been found nearby. Centuries of filling swamps and redirecting waterways have concealed the swamp's watery past, but nearby roads still flood during heavy rainstorms.

In the nineteenth century, industrious Yankees began harvesting ice from Fresh Pond, shipping their frozen harvest as far as Singapore. By the 1850s, there were thirty-five ice houses by the pond. Fresh Pond began to supply Cambridge's drinking water then, and Fresh Pond itself became a bucolic day trip for city-weary Bostonians. Unfortunately, the rest of the Great Swamp gradually became an industrial wasteland; all the unpleasant businesses that supply cities—slaughterhouses, tanneries, glue factories, and other smelly manufacturers—were located near Fresh Pond's shores. Sewage from the ice houses' workers and horses seeped into the water supply as well. In 1879, Cambridge annexed five hundred and seventy acres (and six hundred residents) of Belmont surrounding Fresh Pond to protect the reservoir. In the 1880s, there were several malaria outbreaks in the neighborhood around the pond. Finally, in 1889, the Massachusetts state legislature gave Cambridge the right by eminent domain to take all land surrounding Fresh Pond in order to protect the reservoir.

A new park was designed for the site in 1897 by Charles Eliot and the Olmsted Brothers. That firm was founded by Frederick Law Olmsted's sons, who took up their father's mantle. Over the next fifteen years, the new park was planted with over one hundred thousand plants, including twenty-five thousand white pines, three thousand hemlocks, and about eighteen hundred willows. In the 1920s and 1930s, Cambridge erected a city infirmary (now Neville Place Nursing Home) on top of a scenic overlook and replaced a meadow and carriage trails with a golf course—very few Cambridge residents were using a horse and carriage by the 1930s.

Like many great urban parks, Fresh Pond was nearly loved to death. Over the park's first century, many of the Olmsteds' trees grew into magnificent giants—a draw for the public, whose use of the park compacted soil and caused erosion around paths. The site's woods became overrun with invasive shrubs and vines that destroy native plant communities and shade out tree seedlings. Cambridge began an ambitious project in the late 1990s to restore Fresh Pond Reservation's ecological health.

The most intensive restoration work took place at the Northeast Sector, the area of the reservation bordering Concord Avenue at the intersection with Alewife Brook Parkway. Work crews removed invasive shrubs and trees and hand-thinned some native trees to provide enough room for the remaining trees to grow. Instead of shredding or burning the pruned branches of native trees though, the branches were used to create "log bars" and bundles of live branches (also called fascines) to stabilize slopes. These barriers form low walls that slow runoff stormwater. Instead of rushing down the slope, eroding the earth, and carrying pollutants toward Fresh Pond, the runoff now pools and sinks into the earth behind the log bars and brush barriers. Some of the log bars have sprouted saplings as well, holding even more earth in place. The slopes were also sprayed with a compost and mulch mixture seeded with native grasses and shrubs, like little bluestem grass and dogwoods.

Closer to the pond, Lusitania Field has been transformed from a soccer field to a four-acre stormwater-treatment wetland. Stormwater that once gushed across the field in sheets now seeps into soil under native wetlands plants like Joe Pye weed. The plants' roots filter out contaminants in the stormwater and reduce erosion; the plants provide valuable habitat for birds and other creatures. Recently the city introduced a biocontrol project for the invasive wetlands plant purple loosestrife by releasing thousands of *Galerucella* beetles to nibble at the plants around the pond.

Next to Neville Place, the city installed a two-acre butterfly meadow over a former parking lot. Filled with native plants, including echinacea, asters, goldenrods, and other nectar-producing plants, the meadow glows with purple and gold in late summer.

Today, Fresh Pond Reservation is a diverse and busy place. Mature woods, open meadows, and water attract an enormous variety of resident and migrating birds; the Friends of Fresh Pond's bird checklist features over one hundred and twenty species. Visitors to the Northeast Sector woods can find century-old oaks, sycamores, maples, and hickories planted as part of the Olmsted Brothers' design. Below those mighty trees are native understory plants, including winterberry, pagoda dogwood, musclewood, and gray dogwood. In the Kingsley Park area, a great swath of southwest facing lawn for sunning and napping, visitors can enjoy the park's brighter disposition. Dogs can enjoy a swim at Little Fresh Pond, near the golf course on the west side of the pond, but there has been talk of permits for off-leash dogs; check with the city before you let Rover have a swim. In any case, don't let Rover (or children) run next to the fence by the water of the big pond; the pond's perimeter is infested with poison ivy. Keep the water pure and your skin itch free by staying on the path.

Charles River Esplanade (Charles River Reservation)

Charles River from Leverett Street to the BU Bridge (Boston side); O'Brien Highway to BU Bridge (Cambridge side)
617-626-1250
www.mass.gov/dcr; Search: Charles River
Open all year, dawn to dusk
Handicap accessible
Free

The Esplanade is Boston's glory on the Charles, a place to spend a summer day admiring a grand river flecked with sailboats, crew shells, and candy-colored amphibious Duck Boats. Young adventurers will enjoy romping across small bridges to man-made islands and lagoons. Paved paths attract plenty of bicyclists and joggers—but beware, once you start exploring the Esplanade, you may find yourself going much farther than you had planned. This riverfront park is merely the first and most famous segment of the Charles River Reservation, which continues for another seventeen miles upstream from the BU Bridge.

Like the Public Garden and the Back Bay Fens, the Esplanade was once a sewage-strewn tidal mudflat. Boston built a ten-acre park for residents of Boston's West End tenements near the mouth of river in the 1880s, but the Charles River's banks were not transformed into a hygienic pleasure ground until the project that dammed the Charles River in 1905–1910. The chief proponent of the dam was banker James Jackson Storrow, who envisioned

a new Charles River basin as a beautiful park for walking and boating.

The Charles River Dam turned the lower Charles from a tidal mudflat to a fresh-water lake. Gravel and mud dredged from the river bottom covered the polluted flats and created land for a new park that became known as the "Esplanade," from a French term for a walkway next to water. Alas, the new park was an immediate flop. Few cared to promenade on this narrow, sun-baked strip of grass and concrete, and the new vertical seawalls made the waves too rough for most boating. The place was almost deserted.

Fortunately, a Storrow once again intervened. After her husband's death in 1926, Helen Storrow donated $1 million to the city to improve the park. With additional money from the state and city, forty new acres of land were built between the dam and what is now the BU Bridge. Arthur Shurcliff designed the new park, adding a lagoon along the river between Exeter and Fairfield Streets, sloping seawalls and breakwaters to tame the waves, and a lawn with a band shell (now known as the Hatch Shell). Shurcliff also added over a thousand trees and twelve thousand shrubs, making the hot strip into a shady bower.

Unfortunately, riverside real estate was valued for more than just a pedestrian promenade. Storrow Drive wiped out acres of Esplanade parkland for a highway, built in 1951. The octogenarian Shurcliff worked with his son to repair the damage. They created a new island and another lagoon on the Boston side of the river.

Today, Bostonians of all ages enjoy the Esplanade. Community Boating, the nation's oldest public sailing program, runs programs for adults and youth from a dock near Longfellow Bridge. Their activity gives joy to sailors and admiring onlookers. In the spring, the park is bright with pink cherry blossoms and graceful yellow-green willows. All sorts of festivals are held here: the largest is the Fourth of July fireworks and Boston Pops orchestra concert, which attracts hundreds of thousands of people every year. A giant sculpted head of Arthur Fiedler, a beloved Pops conductor, nods toward the Hatch Shell from the Esplanade's banks—a pleasant place to spend eternity.

Walden Pond State Reservation

915 Walden Street (Route 126), Concord
978-369-3254
www.mass.gov/dcr/parks/walden
Open in summer, 7:00AM–8:00PM; other seasons, 7:00AM–7:00PM
Selected areas handicap accessible, beach wheelchairs available
Parking fee is $5 per vehicle; parking closes when lot reaches capacity in the summer. Call main number to check parking status

"When I wrote the following pages, or rather the bulk of them, I lived alone, in the woods, a mile from any neighbor, in a house which I had built myself, on the shore of Walden Pond, in Concord, Massachusetts, and earned my living by the labor of my hands only. I lived there two years and two months. At present I am a sojourner in civilized life again." So begins Henry David Thoreau's *Walden, or Life in the Woods,* a journal of his thoughts and experiences as he lived in a small cabin in the woods from 1845 to 1847. Today, the pond and its surrounding forest is a popular destination for summer swimming and autumn walks, attracting over six hundred thousand visitors a year.

Walden Pond State Reservation consists of a sixty-acre pond with a bathhouse and swimming beach

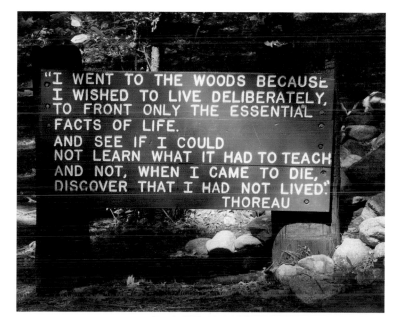

"I WENT TO THE WOODS BECAUSE
I WISHED TO LIVE DELIBERATELY,
TO FRONT ONLY THE ESSENTIAL
FACTS OF LIFE.
AND SEE IF I COULD
NOT LEARN WHAT IT HAD TO TEACH
AND NOT, WHEN I CAME TO DIE,
DISCOVER THAT I HAD NOT LIVED."
THOREAU

surrounded by 462 acres of woods; the visitor center is located across the street. The pond is 103 feet deep, a glacial kettle pond formed when a chunk of a glacier melted on the spot ten thousand years ago. The pond is renewed by local groundwater, and no rivers or streams flow in or out of the pond. The entrance to the reservation from the parking lot brings visitors to a swimming beach and bathhouse, with showers and changing areas, and the beginnings of the walking trails that ring the pond.

Thoreau's writings on self-reliance, simple living, and his careful, rapturous descriptions of the nature surrounding him inspired generations of environmentalists and activists the world over, but local farmers did not find his actual house inspirational. In 1849, Thoreau's cabin was moved to another site in Concord, where it was used to store grain and eventually dismantled. Today, a replica of the cabin stands at the edge of the eco-friendly parking lot (the lot is made of permeable pavement, which allows stormwater to trickle into the ground below). Contemporary Transcendentalists place stones at the original cabin site on the far edge of the pond in simple homage to the sage of Walden.

Walden Pond has a long history of human use. When Thoreau built his cabin, the land around Walden Pond was a wood lot—a patch of trees kept to provide firewood and building materials—located less than a half-hour walk outside of town. Far from a pristine wilderness, the Walden woodlots had previously housed local slaves, servants, and railway workers, and Thoreau comments in *Walden* on the smell of a dead horse left in a nearby abandoned cellar hole. Concord's residents fished, hunted, and picked berries in the woods; the pond was used for swimming, skating, and harvesting ice. The track for the Fitchburg railroad line was laid near the pond a year before Thoreau moved in, and in 1866, the railroad built an amusement

park on Walden's shores. The park burned down in 1902 and was never rebuilt. Still, visitors kept coming: by 1917 there were bathhouses, and the pond attracted over two thousand summer visitors a day. Local residents sensitive to the site's heritage began working to preserve the woods in 1922; the pond became a National Historic Landmark in 1965 and a state park in 1975.

All this enthusiasm for nature took its toll, and in 1996, Walden Pond underwent a massive landscape restoration and erosion control project. The Bioengineering Group of Salem, MA, stabilized over three thousand feet of shoreline by using forty-five species native trees, shrubs, grasses, and flowers as tools to hold soil in place. Landscapers put in sod, containing low-bush blueberry plants, beside trails and planted live stakes of tree cuttings through coconut-fiber coir blankets to stabilize slopes. Remains of the coconut fibers can still be seen near the pond today. On eroded slopes, they used brush layering, an overlapped crisscrossing of willow and dogwood branches under a layer of soil. The branches' growing tips were exposed and grew into shrubs, while the branches themselves grew roots and held the soil in place on the slope. The restoration project has been amazingly successful given how intensely the site is used, and the trails through the woods still look like paths, despite the pedestrian highways they become on sultry summer days.

The landscape around the pond is mostly oak-hickory woods, with low-bush blueberries, sheep laurel, and other small shrubs on the forest floor. The site is varied though, and visitors can find white birches, smooth-trunked beeches, and dark groves of eastern hemlock in the woods. An American chestnut on the property has flowered in recent years, providing valuable nuts to the American Chestnut Foundation's effort to restore blight-resistant trees to the American landscape. The pond is stocked for fishing, and a variety of birds enjoy the pond as a resting place in their migrations.

Not all is well with Walden though. As one of America's first ecologists, Thoreau kept detailed botanical notes on the pond, recording the date of first flowering for several hundred species of plants for eight years. Using Thoreau's notes in 2008, scientists from Harvard and Boston Universities found that the mean annual temperature in Concord has risen by four degrees since Thoreau sojourned at the pond, and the forty-three flowers Thoreau recorded most consistently are blooming a week earlier than in Thoreau's time. More worrisome is their finding that 27 percent of the 473 plant species Thoreau painstakingly described in *Walden* have disappeared, and 36 percent are in danger of extinction from the site. If you wish to celebrate Thoreau's legacy, consider doing so without exacerbating global warming: ride there on a bike. See the Minuteman Bikeway, chapter 14, for one suggested route.

Charles River Watershed Association

From sponsoring kayak races to identifying illegal dump sites, the Charles River Watershed Association (CRWA) works to revitalize the Charles River. The group was founded in 1965, when the Charles River was in a sorry state from decades of unregulated dumping. The river was unswimmable, and anyone who had the misfortune to fall in was supposed to get a tetanus shot.

Over the past four decades, the CRWA has been hard at work collaborating with hydrologists, urban planners, wetlands scientists, and other experts to keep pollution from entering the river in the first place and to protect the river and its banks for future generations. The CRWA's mission is "to use science, advocacy, and the law to protect, preserve, and enhance the Charles River and its watershed," but the association also uses old-fashioned muscle for park cleanups. They host the annual Run of the Charles canoe and kayak race too.

To help the CRWA keep the Charles's waters clear and its parks green, see www.crwa.org.

4.　Big Dig Parks: Making the New City Green

THANKS TO THE BIG DIG'S SINKING BOSTON'S CENTRAL ARTERY highway underground, the city has gained over three hundred acres of open space in the last two decades. The parks are still evolving: pavilions, museums, and other amenities are planned for several sites along the Rose Fitzgerald Kennedy Greenway, and it will take years before the planted saplings will reach their full grandeur. Your opportunity to see a new park's bones, the structures and edges that will be softened and hidden in a few years with branches and leaves—and to remember just how degraded the land was just two decades ago—is now. Stand in the middle of the greenway, look at the bees sucking nectar from a brown-eyed Susan, and revel that in 1990, that very spot was under a road carrying about one hundred and ninety thousand vehicles a day. The greenway is a man-made wonder, and a wonderful place to look up and see the sky. From Paul Revere Park to Chinatown's vermilion gates, the Big Dig's green spaces feature innovative fountains, curving paths, and brilliant flowers.

LEFT: DEWEY SQUARE PARK. ABOVE: MILLENNIUM PARK.

Paul Revere Park

Charles River between North Washington Street Bridge (Route 99) and Zakim Bridge (Route 93)
617-626-1250
www.bostonharborwalk.com; Search: Paul Revere Park
Open all seasons, dawn to dusk
Handicap accessible
Free

One great feature of Paul Revere Park is an unparalleled view of the Zakim Bridge, also known as the "Wishbone Bridge" to locals. Alas, to acquire that view puts visitors almost directly under Route 93, one of the busiest highways in Boston—a bit wearisome to folks not enamored of motor vehicles.

Paul Revere Park features a large, grassy oval where neighborhood dog owners come to let their pooches romp, a small playground, and decorative mosaics on some park walls and on a swirling cylindrical monument. Energetic walkers may enjoy crossing from Charlestown over to Boston via the neighboring Charles River Dam and Locks. The dam walkway features local artist Paul Matisse's *Charlestown Bells*, an interactive artwork made of crayon-colored pipes passers-by can hit to make noise.

Rose Fitzgerald Kennedy Greenway

Along Purchase Street/Surface Artery Road from North Street to South Station
617-292-0020 | www.rosekennedygreenway.org
Parks open daily, 7:00AM–11:00PM; pedestrians may use parks at any time
Handicap accessible
Free

A ribbon of green in the city, the Rose Fitzgerald Kennedy Greenway is a lovely, controversial response to the elimination of the elevated highway that split Boston fifty years ago. Today, instead of a highway, there is a street of green between Surface Road and Cross Street/Atlantic Avenue comprising nearly thirty acres of reclaimed land. Supporters delight in this series of city parks with pleasant places to stroll or sit near fountains and flowers near downtown offices and popular tourist spots; critics claim that the greenway is awkward and stuffed between streets and skyscrapers, a place for office workers to eat lunch and nothing more.

For now, the greenway is open and unsheltered; years from now, it will be a tree-lined boulevard where trees and shrubs grown to their full height shade the streets. Despite the controversy, one group wholeheartedly supports the greenway: bees. The blooms of native plants along the Wharf District and Dewey Square Parks attract bees, butterflies, and other hungry bugs. On a sunny summer day, the quieter parts of the greenway hum with thousands of wings, a joy for budding entomologists.

The greenway's contentious history is almost as long as the park itself. For over twenty years, this landscape snaking from the North End to Chinatown was under Boston's central artery (Route 93), an elevated highway that separated Boston from its waterfront, constructed between 1951–1959. Navigating Boston by foot was a tricky business: visitors who wanted to cross from Faneuil Hall to the North End had to pick their way through a dark, unpleasant underpass. Although this section of the highway was just one-and-a-half miles long, poor design led to unending traffic snarls as the number of users surged from seventy-five thousand vehicles per day in 1959 to one hundred and ninety thousand per day by 1990.

In 1982, the city began planning the now-infamous Big Dig, a colossal construction project to sink the central artery below ground. Strangely, plans for just what to do with the newly exposed land languished. Debates over who was responsible for some parcels, unsuccessful fundraising, and broken contracts delayed development. Some of the grandest plans for the greenway remain undeveloped—a botanical conservatory called the Garden Under Glass, a Harbor Park pavilion for visitors to the Harbor Islands, a museum, an arts center. Time will tell which of these projects will come to fruition.

The greenway officially opened on October 4, 2008. The park consists of several distinct properties bounded by cross streets, but the properties can be grouped into three sites: the North End Parks, the Wharf District Parks, and the Dewey Square Parks.

A few of the sites have proper names, but the parks also bear the titles of Parcels 1 to 23, running from north to south along Surface Road. Parcels 1–7 and 9–12 are zoned for vents and other support structures for the subterranean highway.

The **North End Parks** (Parcels 8–10) run from New Sudbury Street to North Street and link the North End with Faneuil Hall, Haymarket, Government Center, and the Freedom Trail.

The west side of the North End parcels consists of formal perennial gardens of irises, peonies, and poppies edged with boxwood hedges. When they come into their full glory, young red maples will shade the sidewalks and ornamental pears will bloom along cross streets. The center of these parcels features large expanses of lawn for sitting or play. The most popular feature of these parks is the oversized steel pergolas running along the east side of the New Sudbury Street and Hanover Street parcels. Shading plenty of benches and cafe chairs, these pergolas will be covered with vines someday. For now, visitors will simply have to enjoy their view of a line of fountains below the pergolas' plaza, a series of ground-level water spouts crowded with young bathers in summer months.

Neighboring Parcel 9 (North Street to Commercial Street) is slotted to become the Boston Museum someday. Parcel 13 (between Commercial/Clinton Street and Atlantic Avenue Extension) will one day contain a memorial to the Armenian genocide.

The **Wharf District Parks** run from Atlantic Avenue Extension past Christopher Columbus Park and the New England Aquarium to High Street (Parcels 14–17). These parks feature wide lawns, large paved plazas to accommodate groups visiting the waterfront, and diverse plantings of ornamental grasses and perennials. The North End's red maples give way to London plane trees along Surface Road here, and honey locusts mark the cross streets. Past India Street, the greenway becomes quieter. The crowds dwindle, the pavement narrows. The city side still has tight, formal plantings here—but the harbor side is wilder. Parcel 17, between India Street and High Street, is one of the best places around town to observe nectar-collecting insects. The native perennial plantings there include Joe Pye weed, black cohosh, blazing star, yarrow, *Agastache*, asters, and butterfly weed—a smorgasbord for our six-legged friends. The gardens also host red maple trees, sweet gums, and cockspur hawthorns and native shrubs, including winterberry, red osier dogwood, and blueberries.

If you look carefully, you will detect features that link the parks to the sea. Images of fish and trade routes are carved into granite stones, and Parcel 17's paving stones are engraved with observations about life in the United States from immigrants who arrived in Boston's ports over the last three centuries. Rugged salvaged granite stones from Boston's seawalls edge plantings and provide attractive, if uncomfortable, seating.

The most prominent nod to the sea at Parcel 15 (State Street to Milk Street) is a wave fountain. A series of ground-level jets spurt water up to thirty feet high, then it collapses in a choreographed dance. The pulses are just irregular enough to surprise and confuse some very wet children who gather there in summer months. The line of rising and falling plumes of water becomes a tide of light when illuminated from below in the evenings. Parcels 15 and 16 also contain "light blades," vertical sculptures that evoke flags, or sails, or perhaps buoys warning you not to fall into Surface Road.

Parcel 18 between High Street and Oliver Street has been designated the future home for the New

WHARF DISTRICT PARK.

Center for Arts and Culture, a project of the Combined Jewish Philanthropies and the Jewish Community Centers of Greater Boston. This four-story, 80,000-square-foot exhibition, conference, and performance space designed by architect Daniel Liebeskind is supposed to open in 2012.

The **Dewey Square Parks** run from Seaport Boulevard/Evelyn Moakley Bridge to South Station (Parcels 19–22). The Massachusetts Horticultural Society had intended to place a grand Garden Under Glass conservatory on the site, but they failed to raise the funds to actually build it. The Boston Redevelopment Authority (BRA) is starting a new planning process to decide these parcels' ultimate fate. For now, stone pavement gives way to stonedust paths, and the most obvious architectural features here are large square planters filled with showy plants like caladiums and lime green sweet potato vines.

Still, visitors can enjoy gardens planned by Halvorson Design. The complete Halvorson garden design, including plant lists, is available on the Massachusetts Horticultural Society website, www.masshort.org/Gardens-Design.

As the Massachusetts Horticultural Society states on its website, "The gardens are anchored by numerous award winning shrubs and perennials that have stood the test of time." The plants are familiar, bright, and charming; most are either New England native or have won gold medals for excellence from various horticultural societies. Expect strong contrasts of color and foliage texture in this site. Although there are many native plants here, it is emphatically a flower garden, not a natural landscape.

DEWEY SQUARE PARK.

Parcel 19's undulating paths are framed by perennials, including anemones, coneflower, coreopsis, phlox, daylilies, and 'Rozanne' geraniums. Native shrubs, including sweet pepperbush, red-twig dogwood, and low-bush blueberries, are sprinkled through the site. Parcel 21 features more spring-blooming perennials, adding peonies and poppies to the planting mix along with late-summer asters and goldenrod. The colorful palette is rounded out with hydrangeas, roses, and tree peonies. A large round center lawn takes up most of this parcel. Parcel 22 has the simplest plantings, as the site is dominated by a large vent building. Boxwoods surround polyantha roses, and hollies shelter plants, including bee-balm, yarrow, hardy geraniums, and Joe Pye weed.

The Dewey Square Parks' lawns are being maintained using only organic techniques by Safelawn through 2010. Feel free to roll in the grass.

Chinatown Park

Essex Street at Surface Road, Boston
www.rosekennedygreenway.org
Open twenty-four hours; fountain runs spring–fall, 9:00AM–9:00PM
Handicap accessible
Free

CHINATOWN PARK.

Enter through the Chinatown Park's grand red steel gate, and you will wander into a small, soothing oasis of soft bamboo, water, and gray stones. Built on top of a former highway on-ramp, this one-acre park at the edge of Boston's Chinatown leads strollers on a journey down a winding path next to a river-fountain and a waterfall flowing over rough-cut granite blocks. These stones are reclaimed from sea walls, part of the Boston wharfs where many East Asian immigrants arrived. You can't see exactly where you're going when you enter Chinatown here; you must follow the curving path and wait for your destination to be revealed.

At the park's boundaries, towering red cages protect feathery pale green bamboo—a striking contrast of hard and soft, bright and pale—and a wall's wavy top reflects the themes of water and travel. Below, the park features Asian-themed plantings of azaleas, peonies, and cherries bursting with cheerful blooms in the spring, as well as black pine and gingko trees. At night the bamboo plantings are illuminated from below, making green-glowing lanterns to light your way. The walkway's paving stones are arranged to look like dragon scales and continue into a large open plaza featuring an in-ground Chinese chess board.

Millennium Park

398 Gardner Street (near VFW Parkway), Boston
617-635-4505
www.newtonconservators.org/25millennium.htm
Open all year, dawn to dusk
Some areas handicap accessible
Free

Millennium Park is one hundred acres of vast open spaces, intriguing wetlands, and delightful views of Boston and the Charles River. Take a moment to look at the sky as well: Millennium Park is one of Boston's best destinations to watch birds and kites.

Technically, Millennium Park was not built as part of the Big Dig—it was built *from* the Big Dig. Tons of dirt and fill scooped out from under Boston were piled on top of the former Gardner Street Landfill to create a towering one-hundred-acre park.

The park's center is, well, a gigantic mound covered with twenty-one acres of sports fields, a playground, picnic areas, and the park's two portable toilets. The edges are where the park gets interesting. The city is invisible, the views of nature deep and wide. The sides of the great mound are covered with meadow grasses and wildflowers, including delicate goldenrods and New England asters. Walk around the west side of the park to find the Charles River frontage, a wild, forested area with a nature trail and a canoe launch. From there, follow the Nature Study Path counterclockwise to find the Sawmill Brook and a vast marshy area filled with cattails. All these different habitats and fresh water make the park a magnet for birds (and birders).

A small bridge from the Nature Study Path will take you through second-growth woods to Brook Farm Historic Site or the Charles River Path to Cutler Park. In the fall, the trails are dotted with enough wood asters to look like a New England fairy banquet.

Brook Farm Historic Site

While beautiful, Brook Farm's 179 acres of meadows, fields, and forest are not unique. This park's distinction is its past occupants. From 1841 to 1847, some of New England's most prominent Transcendentalists and other thinkers attempted to create a perfect communal society on this site. Residents included Nathaniel Hawthorne, George Ripley, and Charles Dana; frequent visitors included Ralph Waldo Emerson, Margaret Fuller, Bronson Alcott, Theodore Parker, and Horace Greeley.

Unitarian minister George Ripley and ten other investors bought the farm in 1841. Ripley wrote that the Brook Farm commune would be "devoted to industry without drudgery, and true equality without its vulgarity." Every Brook Farm resident was expected to work a variety of jobs at the farm, from milking cows to teaching in a communal school, but all were paid the same wages. It was a radical experiment in equality for men, women, laborers, and intellectuals, and the Brook Farm commune had a profound effect on nineteenth century social movements ranging from abolitionism to women's rights.

Over time thirty-two people joined the Brook Farm experiment. Alas, West Roxbury's thin soil was not nearly productive enough to support the group. The farm's financial stresses were exacerbated when the commune's nearly completed central hall burned to the ground in March 1846, and the group dissolved shortly afterwards. It took Ripley thirteen years to pay off Brook Farm's debts.

Not much is left of the Brook Farm experiment on the site. Some stone foundations remain, but the single historic building in the park is an 1890s print shop, a remnant of a Lutheran orphanage on the site. A path leads past the neighboring Gethsemane Cemetery to Millennium Park and the Charles River Reservation. Transcendentalists reveled in the power of man's connection to God through nature; take the time to renew your own spirit in this peaceful place.

Enter the Brook Farm Historic Site at 670 Baker Street in West Roxbury.

OPPOSITE: MILLENNIUM PARK.

5.   Pocket Parks

SMALL CAN BE BEAUTIFUL. TUCKED AWAY BETWEEN BUILDINGS and busy streets, Boston area pocket parks are respites, exquisite green sculptures carved out of concrete, asphalt, and stone. Though maybe not grand enough to merit a special trip—they lift your spirits when you happen upon them. Pocket parks are places to pause, to reflect, to admire, to breathe.

The shaded plaza at the North End's Paul Revere Mall provides calm in Boston's North End. A statue of a bird dominates the Garden of Peace, a memorial park just steps from Government Center. The exquisitely maintained park in Post Office Square is chock-a-block with lunching office workers on summer weekdays. If crowds tire you, a Japanese-inspired garden at the Museum of Fine Arts allows visitors to contemplate the changing seasons in a serene city oasis; Ramler Park is a bird sanctuary in Boston's busy Fenway; and Hall's Pond Sanctuary in Brookline commonly has more visible fish and frogs than people. Library pocket parks also offer space for quiet contemplation—with fountains and soaring arches at the Boston Public Library Central Branch, arching serviceberry trees at the Honan-Allston Branch, and whimsical stretching cat benches at the Valente Library garden in Cambridge. Franklin Street Park is a quiet oasis near Cambridge's bustling Central Square. All these places are sublime, and not far away.

LEFT: HALL'S POND SANCTUARY. ABOVE: PAUL REVERE MALL.

Paul Revere Mall (Prado)

Freedom Trail between Unity and Hanover
Streets (behind Old North Church), North End
617-635-4505
Open all year, dawn to dusk
Handicap accessible
Free

Paul Revere rides again—through a brick-paved urban allée shaded by linden trees and cooled by a grand fountain. The bronze statue, by sculptor Cyrus Dallin, of Revere and his stalwart horse majestically galloping away from the Old North Church is the park's focal point. Shielded from the North End's bustle by high brick walls yet wide enough to accommodate hundreds of unhurried visitors, the Paul Revere Mall feels like a venerable European city square—even though it wasn't built until the 1930s.

This small park was known as the Prado when it was first built. Legend has it that Boston mayor James

Michael Curley was inspired to create it after seeing Spain's Prado Museum. Curley had three-quarters of an acre of North End tenements demolished to build the park, which opened in 1933. At the time, the state had strict controls in place over Boston city taxes and budgets, so all this destruction and creation was funded by the George Robert White Fund, a private foundation.

The park was designed by Arthur Shurcliff, the prominent landscape architect who also created portions of the Charles River Esplanade, renovated the Back Bay Fens, and was one of the Bostonians credited with devising Boston's most famous ring road—Route 128. A fountain was installed in 1934; the statue of Paul Revere arrived in 1940, and the park was renamed. The park's brick walls display thirteen plaques dedicated to veterans, famous buildings, statesmen, and other historical figures.

The park is an elegant urban space, and a cool respite from the crowds along the Freedom Trail and the North End's narrow streets. Neighborhood residents sit and play checkers while tourists stroll and children chase pigeons. Paul Revere would certainly have a pleasant time riding his horse through the mall—but he'd have to ask a lot of people to move out of his way.

Garden of Peace

100 Cambridge Street, Boston
www.gardenofpeacememorial.org
Open all year, dawn to dusk
Handicap accessible
Free

You could walk on Cambridge Street a thousand times and never realize you were so close to so many memories. Tucked away behind Cambridge

Street's frenzied traffic is the Garden of Peace, where Massachusetts's victims of homicide are remembered in a river of stones.

The landscape is simple, almost spare; the park's focal points are two sculptures and the dry river, not the plants. The park's path begins at *Tragic Density*, a large black orb made of polished black granite set at the highest point in the park. Landscape designer Catherine Melina said that when she imagined the pain felt by parents of murdered children, "I felt a burning in my chest as if I had tried to swallow a stone, a stone that … would be visible as a huge orb, ten, twelve feet across." From *Tragic Density* flows a dry river made of smooth brown stones. Hundreds of stones bear the names and dates of death for homicide victims. Stones for John and Robert Kennedy are here; thirty stones bear names of Massachusetts residents who died on September

11; some stones commemorate victims made famous by newspaper stories; other stones commemorate less famous victims who are still desperately missed.

The walkway by the dry river passes through simple plantings of birches and tall grasses that shudder in the wind. The river ends at *Ibis Ascending*, sculptor Judy Kensley McKie's embodiment of three stylized birds taking flight. The entire park is only seven thousand square feet, which hardly seems large enough for all that is stored in the stones.

Paul Rober of Parents of Murdered Children began the Peace Garden project in 1995. Garden of Peace, Inc., was incorporated in 2001, and the park was completed in 2004. Since then, the garden has held annual ceremonies to commemorate the dead. Tragically, every year more stones appear.

Post Office Square
(Norman B. Leventhal Park)

Post Office Square (corner of Milk, Congress,
Pearl, and Franklin Streets)
www.normanbleventhalpark.org
Open all year, 6:00AM–9:00PM
Handicap accessible
Free

A *Boston Globe* critic once reckoned Post Office
Square as "the perfect park in the perfect location
with a perfect design and perfect maintenance."
Also known as Norman B. Leventhal Park, the
site is 1.7 acres of carefully planned, carefully
maintained green space in the heart of Boston's
financial district. Lunching office workers enjoy a
lush lawn, a pavilion with a cafe, a trellis colonnade, a fountain, whimsical sculptures, and stately
shade trees as they stroll past hydrangeas, lilies,
and impatiens—all while standing on the green
roof atop a 500,000-square-foot underground
parking garage.

It was not always so. From the 1950s through
the 1980s, the site was an above-ground parking
garage, privately owned but built on city-owned
land. Developer Norman B. Leventhal looked out
on the property from his newly developed luxury

PERGOLA AND LANDSCAPE ARCHITECTS: THE HALVORSON DESIGN PARTNERSHIP.
FOUNTAIN SCULPTURES: HOWARD BEN TRÉ. ORNAMENTAL FENCE: RICHARD DUCA.

hotel, the Meridien, and decided to improve the view. Leventhal formed the Friends of Post Office Square, a consortium of wealthy businessmen. Together, Leventhal and the Friends of Post Office Square wrested control of the aging garage from its owner and negotiated to lease the land from the city for one dollar a year. The Friends of Post Office Square then created their own underground parking garage and park, which opened in 1990. The fourteen-hundred-space garage reaches eighty feet under the earth, but is nearly invisible from the surface; even the park's eight-foot-tall vent pipes are disguised. A portion of the profits from the garage fund the park's maintenance.

Technically, Post Office Square is a private garden, restricted to patrons of the Friends of Post Office Square, but in practice, it is an extraordinarily successful public park. It is a conservatively designed space, hearkening to Boston's past with brick pavement and a white colonnade. The Arnold Arboretum worked with the Friends of Post Office Square to include plants that were first introduced to the arboretum: climbing hydrangeas, a hardy kiwi vine, a Chinese fleece vine, and the Sargent crabapple. Many of the crabapples persist to this day—unlike the large trees the arboretum donated, which succumbed to the rigors of city life.

Landscape architects at Halvorson Design did a yeoman's job of placing sun-loving flowers and grass in the few areas that aren't shaded much of the day by nearby skyscrapers, and their gardens are blessed with year-round color, from witch hazel to holly. The dome-topped fountain is circled by little trickling jets of water just tall enough to wet the feet of delighted preschoolers. A ring of shade trees around the central lawn provides shelter from the noonday sun, and granite curbs keep the raised lawn from developing messy edges. The pavilion cafe is waiting; why not stay for lunch?

Tenshin-En Garden

Museum of Fine Arts,
465 Huntington Avenue, Boston
617-267-9300 | www.mfa.org
Spring–fall, weather permitting; open daily,
10:00AM–4:00PM
Handicap accessible
Free entry with museum admission

Stone. Tree. Sky. Tenshin-En is a place to contemplate, to see the essence of the few carefully selected plants in an intimate landscape. Built in the style of the Zen temple gardens of fifteenth-century Japan, this 10,000-square-foot space integrates New England plants and stones into a Japanese *karesansui* rock garden design.

Enter through the roofed gate, built in Kyoto, and you will see a spare, open courtyard. The lowest ground is covered with pale gray pebbles that represent water, raked to resemble a river's current and the waves of the sea. A dry waterfall of black stones trickles down a hill, and visitors can walk over granite bridges to visit islands across the stone sea. Over one hundred and fifty boulders have been placed in the garden, providing a contrast of size and texture with the pebbles and greenery.

The plantings are calm, not showy; you won't find urns of day-glow orange marigolds here. American native plants, like mountain laurels, join traditional Japanese garden plants, including Japanese maples, cherry trees, pines, and azaleas. They give the garden a different focus each season, from buds to blooms to bright autumn leaves to the ghost-limbs of winter. This garden is a place to watch the cycles of life.

David and Dorothy Ramler Park

133 Peterborough Street, between
Kilmarnock and Park Drive, Boston
Open all year, dawn to dusk
Handicap accessible
Free

The last time you walked around Boston's Fenway, did you think, "My, it smells good here"? And did you bring a pair of binoculars with you? Diminutive Ramler Park is resplendent with flowers planted to attract birds that might be visiting the Fens and Victory Gardens or following the Muddy River. Since 2004, over two hundred species of birds have visited the site—which seems to have nearly as many varieties of flowers as fliers: bee balm, Oriental poppies, butterfly weed, beach goldenrod, rudbeckias, salvias, veronica, catnip, and roses, just to name a few.

For decades Ramler Park was Ramler Parking Lot, a neglected piece of pavement owned by local businessman David Ramler. The Ramlers donated the site to the city of Boston in the late 1990s, and the Friends of Ramler Park raised funds from the city and private donors to unpave the parking lot and create paradise. Members of the local community requested a park without a playground—one only with plants that would attract birds.

Today, Ramler Park is a semi-wild success. The park is framed by white pines, sweet gums, and magnolias, with shrub plantings of cranberry viburnums, bayberries, blueberries, dogwoods, crabapples, and hawthorns. All of these plants and the flowers provide delicious petals, seeds, and fruit for hungry birds.

Mounds and mounds of blooms billow onto stonedust paths around a small central lawn. A semicircular white pergola stands at one end of the lawn's long axis; a black fountain crowns the other end. From the right angle, the fountain seems to balance the pergola in space. Brilliant blue benches scattered through the park emphasize that the park is full of energy—flying, perching, hopping birds, blooming plants, and countless volunteers who tend the astonishing array of flowers and foliage. This place is always beautiful, and it's simply gorgeous in the late summer when many perennials blossom.

Just in case the birds didn't understand that the park was designed for them, sculptor John Tagiuri welcomes all visitors with *Bird Fence*, a black wrought-iron fence made of silhouettes of dozens of swooping black swallows. How could any two-legged being resist?

Hall's Pond Sanctuary

1120 Beacon Street/Amory Street, Brookline
617-730-2088
www.brooklinema.gov; Search: Hall's Pond
Open all year, dawn to dusk
Handicap accessible
Free

A great blue heron stalks next to a quiet pond, eying a school of minnows shimmering in the water. Nearby, a kingfisher swoops down from its perch in a stately weeping willow. The cattails rustle—some small animal is running near the shore. Welcome to Hall's Pond Sanctuary, five acres of wilderness in the middle of one of Brookline's busiest neighborhoods.

Tucked behind a busy road and a popular ball field, Hall's Pond was once owned by Minna Hall. Hall founded the Massachusetts Audubon Society with her cousin Harriet Hemenway to protect birds and their habitats; she would indubitably be pleased to know that today Hall's Pond is a refuge for great

cedar swamp, all filled in and developed over the past four hundred years. The pond is fed in part by a storm drain that gathers water from one hundred and ten acres of city streets and homes. As part of a renewal project in the late 1990s, the town built a new storm drain filter and constructed two new wetlands areas, cleared thousands of linear feet of invasive vines (primarily multiflora rose, porcelain berry, and Asiatic bittersweet), and installed native plants, shrubs, and trees throughout the sanctuary.

The restoration worked. Cormorants dive, dragonflies flit, a snapping turtle lurks in the mud. This place is not only a sanctuary for them, but for humans as well.

blue herons, kingfishers, and black-crowned night herons among others. The place is full of nourishment for all manner of traveling birds and resident creatures: cattails, pickerel weed, and arrowhead in the water; silver maples, white ash trees, white willows, and weeping willows along the shore; red oaks in the upland woods; and plenty of poison ivy berries for birds—as well as itch-inducing leaves for visitors who stray off the paths.

The town of Brookline bought the property for a park in 1975. Today, Hall's Pond features a boardwalk curling halfway around the pond, making it easy to view painted turtles sunning themselves on logs. Paths lead into the neighboring amory Woods where a white gazebo from a vanished private garden lingers beneath a canopy of trees. Near the Beacon Street entrance, the Friends of Hall's Pond maintains a small formal garden with perennial beds and raised planters.

Although a pond has been at the site since the first Europeans colonized Boston, it has taken a great deal of work to make Hall's Pond look as wild as it does. The site is the last remnant of a very large white

Boston Public Library Courtyard

700 Boylston Street, Boston
617-536-5400 | www.bpl.org
Open all year, Monday–Thursday, 9:00AM–9:00PM; Friday and Saturday, 9:00AM–5:00PM
Handicap accessible
Free

After you've strolled through the Boston Public Library's McKim Building and gawped at the magnificent architecture, stunning murals, and capacious reading rooms, make your way down to the interior courtyard and rest your eyes. There, beyond the high arcade with graceful columns and tables and chairs, is a small formal garden crowned with Frederick MacMonnie's charming *Bacchante and Infant Faun* statue atop a fountain.

This graceful space was modeled on the courtyard at the Renaissance-era Palazzo della Cancelleria in Rome and opened to the public in 1895. The plantings are simple—groundcovers and low boxwood hedges with a few flowers sprinkled here and there—and the garden is small. The entire place feels cooling and peaceful. Visitors can spend the afternoon enjoying the fountain and the quiet green space apart from Copley Square. And don't worry if you forgot to bring a book, the Boston Public Library has 1.7 million more.

Honan-Allston Branch Library

300 North Harvard Street, Allston
617-787-6313
www.bpl.org/branches/allston.htm
Open all year, Monday and Wednesday, noon–8:00PM; Tuesday and Thursday, 10:00AM–6:00PM; Friday, 9:00AM–5:00PM; Saturday and Sunday, closed
Handicap accessible
Free

Behind the striking modern "butterfly" facade, whimsical bicycle racks, and a bustling reference desk, there is a quiet courtyard. Serviceberry trees spread their branches over gray stone, ferns, oakleaf

hydrangeas, and laurels. In the autumn, the trees' delicate leaves glow orange-red. There are chairs and tables where visitors can sit to read, but don't worry if the weather is miserable; you can see the trees through soaring windows from almost anywhere in the library.

The library surrounding the courtyard was built from 2000 to 2001. It went on to win the 2003 Boston Society of Architects' Harleston Parker Medal for "the single most beautiful" building or other structure built in the metropolitan Boston area in the past ten years. Part of the building's charm is its transparency. Enormous windows and a design that alternates rooms and open space mean that patrons can always see two of the library's three courtyards from the central reading rooms: the central courtyard; a "children's courtyard," a stone-paved space under a mature beech tree with sprightly annual flowers in containers; and a small shaded courtyard facing a side street.

The site should become even more interesting in coming years, as there are plans to build a new park in the vacant lot behind the library as part of Harvard University's Allston Initiative to expand into the area. For now, though, you can enjoy the delights of a beautifully designed small space: a place full of light and leaves and the pleasure of the printed word.

Valente Library Reading Garden

826 Cambridge Street (next to Valente Library), Cambridge
617-349-4015
www.cambridgepubliclibrary.org/hours/valente.html
Open all year, dawn to dusk
Handicap accessible
Free

In the middle of one of east Cambridge's busiest streets, where triple-deckers are squeezed tightly to the sidewalk, there is a tiny lush garden prowled by giant bronze cats. Artist Judy McKie created her *Alley Cats* benches expressly for the Valente Library Reading Garden, where they stretch their smooth backs to accommodate passers-by.

The garden itself features spring bulbs and summer perennials, with birches for vertical interest and Juneberries and currant bushes for the birds. Great swaths of echinacea (purple coneflower) bloom in August, while pale boulders rest amid the greenery year-round. The city of Cambridge describes the planting scheme as "Urban Wild," a scheme that includes a few natives amid the daylilies, azaleas, and ivy. Much of the garden space is taken up by pavement, the better to host events and access the library and the street. Still the garden enlivens the street, giving visitors a place to rest, read, and observe city life in an exceptionally crowded part of town. What better way is there to spend the afternoon than to curl up with a book and a cat in a garden?

Franklin Street Park

Franklin Street between Hancock and Bay Streets, Cambridge
617-349-4603
www.cambridgema.gov; Search: Franklin Street Park
Open all year, dawn to dusk
Handicap accessible
Free

Tucked away on a side street near Central Square, Franklin Street Park seems delicate—despite the iron fence, stone-covered walls, and ten-foot-tall granite entrance gate. Sunlight dapples through the high canopy of trees onto a park the size of a small house, illuminating abstract bronze sculptures and sturdy cast-iron chairs. An assortment of seating and tables at different elevations allows users to enjoy the park with friends or sit alone and watch. Neighborhood toddlers come to splash in a small fountain and crawl on a low metal dome, but bigger people use the park for passive recreations: sitting, relaxing, and watching the seasons change in the low beds and tall trees. It is a place for quieting the mind and soul—even in bustling Central Square!

This 4,400-square-foot park was renovated in 2003, and it owes its soothing character to the city of Cambridge and artist Murray Dewart. Dewart collaborated with the city's Office of Community Development to design three sculptures for the park—*Eye of the Buddha*, *Kyrie Gate*, and *Bright Morning*—as well as the entryway, a granite and bronze piece that resembles Japanese torii gates. Dewart also consulted on which trees to thin and where to put paths.

The park's plantings are less ambitious than its built environment. Much of the greenery is pachysandra and creeping juniper, low-maintenance groundcovers that do not overwhelm the sculptures. A few daylilies perk up the entrance in summer months. Still, the consistent, simple textures of pachysandra, granite, and bronze complement each other for a soothing whole.

6.   Urban Wilds

THERE ARE PLACES IN THE CITY WHERE THE PLANTS RUN FREE. THEY aren't carved and contained and shaved into pretty shapes; they're trimmed back from paths, and not much more. That isn't to say that urban wilds aren't maintained. Though volunteers spend thousands of hours each year hauling out trash, pulling up noxious weeds, and putting in new native plants, you won't find the Public Garden's serried rows of color-coordinated tulips in these wilds.

Instead, you'll discover what the city of Boston calls remnants of the original ecosystems that European settlers discovered on the Shawmut Peninsula in 1630: salt marshes at the Belle Isle Marsh Reservation in East Boston, forests in West Roxbury's Allandale Woods, freshwater wetlands at Jamaica Plain's Bussey Brook, and birds at the Boston Nature Center. Boston's fourteen hundred acres of urban wilds are the sort where nineteenth-century Transcendentalists might have looked for clues to God's design.

BOTH PAGES: BELLE ISLE MARSH RESERVATION.

Belle Isle Marsh Reservation

Bennington Street (across from the
Suffolk Downs T stop), East Boston
617-727-5350 | www.mass.gov/dcr; Search:
Belle Isle | www.friendsofbelleislemarsh.org
Open all year, 9:00AM–dusk
Handicap accessible
Free

At Belle Isle Marsh, there are no ball fields, skating rinks, sprinkler parks, or hot dog stands; there is nothing to do but stroll, sit, and feel the rhythms of the earth and sea—and the take-offs from nearby Logan Airport. Between these intermittent interruptions, Belle Isle is one of the most peaceful places in Boston, and a paradise for birds and butterflies.

Belle Isle Marsh is part of the larger Rumney Marshes ecosystem that extends for thousands of acres north through Revere and Saugus. The reservation spans 152 acres of Boston's last remaining salt marsh, as well as fresh-water areas and meadows, with twenty-eight acres of landscaped trails and an observation tower. The upland trails run alongside wildflower meadows and masses of pink rugosa roses, gaudy sweet-scented flowers that thrive in seaside sand and salt spray. Still, most of Belle Isle is salt marsh: a maze of shallow water channels, salt-meadow cordgrass, and phragmites reeds. Muskrats chew secret tunnels through the reeds, and swallows swoop over the grasslands, snatching insects in mid-flight. The place looks vast; an immense antidote to the houses, roads, and airport visible at the reservation's edge.

When the sparkling inlets become mudflats at low tide, the marsh can look downright messy, but eager birds devour the creatures stranded in the sludge. Plenty of herons, egrets, and shorebirds make the rounds at Belle Isle, and bobolinks and meadowlarks stalk the upland grasses. Butterflies and dragonflies also appreciate this grassland by the sea, and robins and mockingbirds frequent the site's few mulberry and wild cherry trees. To get a closer look at the marsh, paddle along on one of the canoe trips sponsored by the Boston Natural Areas Network.

There are no bathrooms or snack bars at Belle Isle, so plan to meet those needs elsewhere. This park belongs to the wild.

Allandale Woods

Bounded by Allandale Street, Centre Street, VFW
Parkway, and Hackensack Road, Jamaica Plain/
West Roxbury
617-635-4505
www.cityofboston.gov; Search: Urban Wilds
Open all year, 9:00AM–dusk
No handicap facilities
Free

There's a hidden world a block away from the Arnold Arboretum. Nearly invisible to passers-by, the ninety-acre Allandale Woods is tucked away behind homes and busy streets. Once you find your way inside, you will have forest, three ponds, a marsh, and dozens of walking trails all to yourself.

Allandale Woods is a second-growth oak-hickory forest. Like most open areas in Greater Boston, the woods were cut for farming and firewood but grew back in the twentieth century. There are remnants of past uses throughout the woods. A six-sided 1870 spring house with a conical roof rests near the Spring House development on Allandale Street, evidence of a natural spring once advertised for its medicinal properties. A long, low stone wall runs from Centre Street into the Allandale Woods.

Unlike most New England stone walls, this wall was built in the 1930s to mark the border between the Brandegee Estate and the city of Boston's property; the estate was later added to the Allandale Woods.

Today, the Allandale Woods is dominated by pignut and shagbark hickories and several varieties of oaks: red, white, black, chestnut, and scarlet. Around wetlands, botanically astute visitors can spot Asian cork trees and castor aralia trees likely planted by birds who had dined at the neighboring Arnold Arboretum. The open woods shelter low-bush blueberries and huckleberries, wood asters, and some astonishing large clumps of bright-orange fungus on fallen trees. There are traces of old farms and estates scattered around the woods—apple trees near the spring house, sugar maples lining the remnants of a curving driveway, crabapples, and ornamental cherries around an old building site.

The trails scamper up and down small hills and cliffs of Roxbury puddingstone, a lumpy-looking composite rock named for steamed fruit-filled puddings of times past. The Appalachian Mountain Club laid out trails in the Allandale Woods in 1992, but they have not been officially maintained, and there are no maps. You're never very far from a busy street here, but it is easy to get lost all the same. Sharp-sighted visitors can find a few signs for the woods and an official entrance to the site behind the Church of the Annunciation on the north side of VFW Parkway near Centre Street.

The most impressive aspect of the Allandale Woods is just how empty it is. A few spots near the edge show signs of past parties, but the place is generally deserted. Everyone is over at the Arnold Arboretum admiring the trees. Come to Allandale Woods to experience a forest instead.

Bussey Brook Meadow

South Street/Forest Hills MBTA Station,
Jamaica Plain
617-556-4110
www.arboretumparkconservancy.org; Search:
Bussey Brook Meadow
Open all year, 9:00AM–dusk
Handicap accessible
Free

ALLANDALE WOODS.

It's a meadow, a wetland, an oak forest, and a tumble of wildflowers—Bussey Brook Meadow is a sunny jumble of sprawling plants and varied microclimates, an interesting foil to the Arnold Arboretum's mannerly plantings next door. In the summer, humming bugs swarm about the blooms and the warm sun gives the place a hazy smell of hay and ponds.

The meadow is named for Benjamin Bussey, the same generous gentleman whose 1842 bequest of land was used to create the Arnold Arboretum. In 1996, the city of Boston, the Arnold Arboretum, and the Arboretum Park Conservancy, a nonprofit group, worked together to add twenty-four acres of land owned by various entities to the arboretum's land lease.

The Blackwell Path, the main walkway through the meadow, was completed in 2002 and runs through the center of the park through a series of meadows. Black oaks and English elms rim the path, and the grassy areas host several butterfly-attracting species: milkweed, goldenrod, clover, tansy, butter-and-eggs, and yarrow. Willows, silver maples, and jewelweeds grow along the wetlands, while cattails and the invasive purple loosestrife march right out of the middle of the muck. The uphill side of the meadow is mostly oak-hickory forest, except for the mesa along the northeast corner, which is populated by an assortment of non-native plants.

Although Bussey Brook is wild, it is hardly untouched. The wetlands were created when the shape of the land was altered by a variety of construction projects, including building the commuter rail line; the mesa is a mound of old construction waste dumped on-site. Since 1996, much of this property has been renovated. Invasive plants have been removed throughout the site (although plenty have reestablished themselves), hundreds of native shrubs and trees have been installed, and the wildflower meadow near the Forest Hills MBTA station is mowed twice a year to keep trees from overwhelming the grasslands.

Despite all that intervention, Bussey Brook still looks and feels wild. No one deadheads spent blooms, and you'll see plenty of signs of aging plants—but you might also see signs of the foxes, wild turkeys, and deer that have been spotted here. If you do go in the summer months, bring insect repellant. After all, mosquitoes are part of the wetlands ecosystem too.

Massachusetts Audubon Boston Nature Center

500 Walk Hill Street, Mattapan
617-983-8500 | www.massaudubon.org;
Search: Boston Nature Center
Nature Center open Monday–Friday, 9:00AM–5:00PM; Saturday, Sunday, and Monday holidays, 10:00AM–4:00PM. Trails open daily, dawn to dusk
Handicap accessible trails and boardwalks
Suggested donation is $2; Massachusetts Audubon members, free

The Boston Nature Center's sixty-seven acres are one of the best places to see red-tailed hawks in Boston. The center's paths wind through majestic trees, a twenty-acre wetland, and the Clark-Cooper Community Gardens. Walks are fairly short—there are just two miles of trails altogether—but the enveloping woods and wildlife leave visitors feeling truly surrounded by nature.

Starting in 1898, this urban forest was part of the grounds of a succession of hospitals; the last facility, the Boston State Hospital, closed in 1979. Apart from the community garden, the grounds languished—allowing all manner of trees and plants to grow as they wished. A botanical survey in the site found one hundred and eighty varieties of plants and trees on the property, including cottonwoods planted around the wetlands in the 1800s. Apart from the variety, the sheer size of some of the trees on the site is simply overwhelming—especially in such an urban location.

For a more calming display, visit the garden by the visitor center, filled with wildlife-friendly plants, like brown-eyed Susan, Joe Pye weed, and *Echinops*. The visitor center itself is a green building, featuring solar panels on the roof, geothermal heating, and columns made from local Roxbury puddingstone; a full rendering of the building's features is available at the center's website.

Wildlife residents include hundreds of snails creeping up plants near the wetlands, coyotes, pheasants, wild turkeys, muskrats, painted turtles, and red-tailed hawks—but the most obvious locals are the red-winged blackbirds. Stand on the wetlands overlook and listen to their cheerful *konk-a-reee!* You'll know that all is right with the world.

BOSTON NATURE CENTER.

The Massachusetts Audubon Society

With one hundred thousand members and thirty-three thousand acres of conservation land, the Massachusetts Audubon Society is a force of nature—yet the society began with hats. In 1896, Harriet Hemenway, a prominent Bostonian matron, read an article about how the craze for plumes on women's hats was destroying America's egret population. Hemenway recruited her cousin Minna Hall, and together these intrepid women set out to convince Boston's entire social register that the slaughter should be stopped. The movement spread rapidly through women's clubs and on to involve civic leaders and scientists throughout the United States.

Today, the Massachusetts Audubon Society leads classes and outings for two hundred thousand children and adults each year and lobbies for better environmental policies at all levels of government. The society also works with individuals and other groups to permanently preserve land from development. The society runs forty-five wildlife sanctuaries, including the Boston Nature Center. Go visit their woods, the native flower garden, and their environmentally friendly building; it's a fine place to hang your hat.

For more information, visit www. massaudubon.org

Boston Natural Areas Network

Next time you're in a wild place thinking, "This can't be in the middle of the city!" take a moment to thank the Boston Natural Areas Network (BNAN). Since 1977, the BNAN has been helping to preserve more than eight hundred acres of Boston's urban wilds, joining with partners to keep land open until it can be legally protected from development.

Over the years the BNAN's mission has expanded to preserve and expand open space by supporting community gardens and greenways as well. The group owns or holds leases on forty Boston community gardens and provides organizational support to more than one hundred and fifty gardens altogether. Since 1995, BNAN has been working with community residents and the government to create greenways along the Neponset River and in East Boston. These linear parks connect communities with green space and provide safe off-road trails for biking and walking. The greenways are still being developed, although portions of the planned parks are open.

To help the BNAN keep Boston green and wild, see www.bostonnatural.org.

Danehy Park

99 Sherman Street, Cambridge
617-349-6200
www.cambridgema.gov; Search: Danehy Park
Open all year, dawn to dusk
Some areas handicap accessible
Free

Danehy Park is a fine place to play softball, climb on a jungle gym, shoot some hoops—or step into the center of a universe. Stroll up a gentle slope into the center of *Turnaround Surround*, an environmental artwork by Mierle Laderman Ukeles, and you can stand on a twenty-four-square-foot dance floor bearing an image of a spiral galaxy. The man-made hill with a panoramic view is a far cry from the site's past as a clay pit and landfill, yet *Turnaround Surround* embodies the land's past degradation and hopeful future.

For over one hundred years, Danehy Park was a gigantic hole in the ground. The New England Brick Company dug clay from the fifty-acre site from 1847 to 1952, when the pit was sold to the city of Cambridge for a landfill. The property served as

Cambridge's dump until the 1970s when the landfill was closed. The city allowed the MBTA to use the site for waste from excavating the new Red Line tunnel from Harvard to Alewife in the 1970s and 1980s, and the park was built on top of these layers of material from 1988 to 1990. Ukeles, artist-in-residence for New York City's Department of Sanitation since 1978, started working on *Turnaround Surround* in 1990.

Turnaround Surround, like the rest of Danehy Park, is made out of trash. The land-sculpture begins with a gentle sloping path made of *glassphalt*, pavement made with asphalt and twenty-two tons of glass scavenged from one week of Cambridge residents' recycling. The pavement glass gleams in sunlight, leading you onward past Ukeles' "smellers and wavers": sweet herbs, roses, and native grasses that belie the site's past foul odors. The view here is briefly blocked by plants; trust the path as it leads you around a blind curve.

At the hill's summit, walkers can rest on two aluminum thrones to show that they are kings of the hill, owners of this public space. From the hilltop, a visitor can look down the slope to the park's great lawn and adjoining wetlands where waves of grasses shimmer in the breeze. More energetic visitors can cavort on the recycled-rubber dance floor to celebrate renewal and healing the land. Buried within the hill are community offerings representing fifty-six different languages and cultures of children in Cambridge public schools. They are "fertilizing the earth with diversity," Ukeles says.

Though it is beautiful, *Turnaround Surround* is not a place for solitary contemplation. The place is alive with birds, buzzing insects, and people—families picnicking, youth sunning themselves, children rolling down the hillside. The green space is filled with activity. It shows that people can reclaim and revitalize degraded land. The wasteland has been returned to life.

Arts on the Point

UMass–Boston
617-287-5347
www.bostonharborwalk.com
Open all year, dawn to dusk
Some areas handicap accessible
Free

UMass–Boston's outdoor sculpture park is sprawling, awe-inspiring, beautiful, and occasionally confusing and decrepit. Don't expect to find a map of the sculptures' locations or consistent labeling. However, this combination of lawns, green roofs, and modernist landscaping is one of the few places in Boston where visitors can view enormous sculptures by contemporary artists, including Roy Lichtenstein, Willem de Kooning, Sol LeWitt, Mark di Suvero, and Luis Jimenez.

At the entrance to UMass–Boston from Morrissey Boulevard, Mark di Suvero's *Huru* comes into view on a stark open lawn—a thirty-foot-tall, thirty-thousand-pound steel tripod with a delicately balanced crown that wobbles in passing breezes. From there, stroll up to the elevated walkway between the Science Center and the McCormack Building in the center of campus to view smaller works, such as Sol LeWitt's *Two Cubes*. Luis Jimenez's *Steelworker* stands before a yards-long concrete planter with small undulating grassy hills and trees. Walking toward

the harbor, you see several unlabeled sculptures, tiny hills, and occasional flower-filled planters that grace UMass–Boston's cement-paved plazas. A stairway at the harbor end of the campus descends to a small native flower bed and to the lawn surrounding Roy Lichtenstein's *Brushstroke Group*, a colorful painted aluminum sculpture poised next to a traffic circle and Dorchester Bay.

UMass–Boston has planned extensive campus renovations and new construction to come over the next decade. Before you visit, be sure to call the campus to check which portions of Arts on the Point are publicly accessible.

Continue walking toward Boston along the Harborwalk next to Dorchester Bay to see a small Japanese garden, framed by a stone gate near the Massachusetts Archives Building, and a circle of

colorful plantings enlivening the drive outside the John F. Kennedy Presidential Library and Museum.

Eastport Park

2 Seaport Lane, Boston
(Across from Commonwealth Pier)
www.bostonharborwalk.com
Open all year, dawn to dusk
Handicap Accessible
Free

Although this small, charming park is full of textural and sculptural delights that are equally playful and striking, the artwork installed here actually prompted a lawsuit on artists' rights to site-specific sculpture. That lawsuit affirmed the site owner's ability to change and remove art that was designed for a particular location. Although David Phillip's granite sculptures—the subject of the lawsuit—ultimately were not removed, there have been subtle changes from the park's original design, including broken sight lines and perspectives that are now concealed behind green leaves. Still, there is much to be admired in this seaport district oasis, with plenty of benches and nooks where visitors can relax, take in the park's whimsy, and contemplate the place of art in public spaces.

The park's art reflects its seaside location. The entrance is announced by Susumu Shingu's *Wind Masters*, a towering yet skeletal abstraction of masts and sails. Below, the park is populated by dozens of maritime creatures sculpted by David Phillips—lobsters crawling up stone benches, tiny frogs guarding planters, scallop shells covering drains, and an enormous hermit crab shell with eyes peeking out from below. Judy Kensley McKie contributed a fish bench, a fanciful bronze Piscean

ARTS ON THE POINT.

that has been chopped clean in half for your seated pleasure.

At the park's center is Phillips's site-specific sculpture *Chords*, a series of smooth spheres, rough stones, and textured pavement defining and breaking through the park's northeast-southwest axis. This sculpture was the subject of a precedent-setting lawsuit. In 2001, Fidelity Investments (which leases the park and surrounding land from the Massachusetts Port Authority) decided to redesign the park to provide more shade and make maintenance easier. Critics said the plan would conceal the park from the street and discourage public use of public property. When artist David Phillips learned that his sculpture would be dismantled, he sued to have it preserved under the Visual Artists Rights Act (VARA). Although the courts ruled that site-specific sculpture was not protected under VARA, Fidelity ultimately left the sculpture and changed the site around it.

The park was once an open landscape that hearkened to the sea, a place with broad vistas planted with oceanside natives: sedums and tall grasses, wild oats and pitch pine. Today, while much of the original flora remains, the site has been overlaid with shade trees and shrubs and a mishmash of decorative flowers, like petunias and miniature daylilies. The revised design lends a mysterious air to *Chords*, which is always partly hidden from view. Subsequently, the park now feels more like a nautical-themed park than an extension of the shoreline.

South Boston Maritime Park

D Street by Northern Avenue, Boston
617-428-2800 | www.bostonharborwalk.com;
Search: South Boston Maritime Park
Open all year, dawn to dusk
Handicap accessible
Free

From a distance, South Boston Maritime Park doesn't look as flashy and fun as neighboring Eastport Park: there aren't nearly as many trees and pretty flowers, no giant mollusks, and the entire place is only 1.3 acres. But cast a careful eye on this landscape. It won the American Society of Landscape Architects 2006 General Design Award of Honor for its careful site planning, sustainable design, and maritime art.

The park's entrance is graced by Carlos Dorrien's *The Gateway*, two large hunks of granite carved with waves, fish, and other life from the sea. The park beyond opens to a lawn and a cafe beneath a high pergola with tall columns recalling masts on the harbor. At the far edge of the park is Ellen Driscoll's *Aqueous Humour*, three great horizontal wheels that turn as passers-by push them to reveal mosaics of marine life, the shipping industry at Conley Terminal, and the fishing industry at Fish Pier. The pavement under these art-go-rounds is engraved with the constellations sailors used for millennia to find their ways across the sea.

That's the grand sculpture scheme—but this park's genius is in the architectural details. The walkway by the entrance is made of paving stones shaped like fish scales. Lights in the walkway by the lawn indicate whether the tide is high or low, and a fog fountain emerges from an oversized lobster-trap. Stones all over the park are carved with tide tables, weather symbols, nautical sayings, and the outline of Boston Harbor. A thirty-five-foot-long tube allows children to talk to someone, well, thirty-five feet away at the other end of the tube. Design enthusiasts will appreciate the grass ramps which allow strollers and wheelchairs easy access to the lawn. Sustainable landscape fans will be happy to know that all the runoff from the cafe's roof flows into an ornamental swale to nourish plants, not into a pipe to burden storm drains.

The park has some plantings sturdy enough to stand the wind and salt spray off the harbor—those hearty garden standbys rugosa roses, brown-eyed Susans, daylilies, and wild oats. With all that is going on here, however, these plantings take second stage to the other features of the park.

Forest Hills Cemetery Contemporary Sculpture Path

95 Forest Hills Avenue, Boston
617-524-0128 | www.foresthillstrust.org
Open all year, 7:30AM–dusk
Some areas handicap accessible
Free

Ghostly translucent nightshirts float through pine trees; a seated woman cast in bronze wears an African headdress and stares at the passing scene; rivers of twigs flow down a forested hillside to a swirling eddy of branches. The Forest Hills Cemetery Contemporary Sculpture Path features dozens of works sprinkled among the 250-acre site's quiet gravestones, shady groves, small hills, grassy lawns, and pond.

The cemetery is not only an elegant park and arboretum but also host to over one hundred and sixty years of memorial art and commissioned sculpture. (See chapter 8 for more information on the history and landscaping at Forest Hills Cemetery.) In the nineteenth century, many patrons commissioned sculptures to mark their graves. The most famous of these artworks is the Milmore Monument, also called *Death Staying the Hand of the Sculptor*, located near the main entrance. The sculpture is a tribute to stonecutter Joseph Milmore and his brother Martin Milmore, a famous sculptor who created the Soldiers and Sailors Memorial on Boston Common, among other works. In this sculpture by Daniel Chester French, an angel of death grabs a sculptor's hand as he brings his chisel up to an unfinished portrait of a sphinx. Forest Hills hosts hundreds of these statues, stones, and other ornaments, making the place an intriguing destination for fans of art history or Victorian culture.

Since the cemetery celebrated its 150th anniversary in 1998, the Forest Hills Educational Trust has been reviving the tradition of cemetery sculpture by hosting annual contemporary sculpture exhibitions on themes such as "Spirits in the Trees" and "The 4 Elements." The selection changes, but some sculptures are retained from year to year, such as Leslie Wilcox's eerie *Nightshirts*, Frank Vasello's *Lethe*, a river of sticks, and Fern Cunningham's *The Sentinel*.

Forest Hills is vast. Pick up a map of the sculpture path at the cemetery entrance if you want to have any chance of locating the art. Compared to Mount Auburn Cemetery or Arnold Arboretum, Forest Hills is slightly out-of-the-way and less popular; you will have plenty of space and quiet here to contemplate the spirits in the trees, the stones, and the ground.

Taylor Square

Taylor Square, Cambridge
617-349-4380 | www.cambridgeartscouncil.org;
Search: Taylor Square
Open all year
Not handicap accessible
Free

Taylor Square isn't a park so much as an idea about parks, access, and ownership. Artist Paul Ramirez Jonas created Cambridge's smallest park, which measures a mere fifty-seven square feet and sits in the middle of a cement-paved plaza in front of the Engine 8, Ladder 4, fire station at the intersection of Garden Street, Huron Avenue, and Sherman Street. The park consists of a small patch

TAYLOR SQUARE.

of lawn, a flagpole, and a bench surrounded by a fence with two locked gates.

In 2005, Jonas installed the park and mailed five thousand keys to the park's gates to Cambridge households along with the following note: "Here is your key. It is one of 5,000 keys that opens Taylor Square, Cambridge's newest park. The park and the keys are a work of public art that I made for you. The park has barely enough room for a bench and a flagpole; please accept this key as its monument. Add it to your key chain along with the keys that open your home, vehicle, or workplace. You now have a key to a space that has always been yours. Copy it and give it away to neighbors, friends, and visitors. Your sharing will keep the park truly open."

Visitors seeking larger green spaces can stroll back down Garden Street to the nearby Longfellow National Historic Site (chapter 15) and the Dr. Paul Dudley White Charles River Bike Path (chapter 14), or take a walk up Sherman Street to Danehy Park.

DeCordova Sculpture Park

51 Sandy Pond Road, Lincoln
781-259-8355 | www.decordova.org
Open all year, Tuesday–Saturday,
10:00AM–5:00PM
Handicap accessible
Adult admission is $12; seniors, students, and children (6–12), $8; children five and under are free

When you visit the DeCordova Sculpture Park, watch your head; sharks might be swimming through the trees. Kitty Wales's *Pine Sharks* is just one of dozens of contemporary artworks that have lurked, stared, or simply sat in the DeCordova's thirty-five acres of hills, lawns, and pond views. The park is chock-full of original sculptures, including a giant wooden piggy (*Trojan Piggy Bank*, Actual Size Artworks) and a vertical marimba which visitors can play with sticks (*The Musical Fence*, Paul Matisse). Between the size of many artworks and the sheer number on display, the place can be a bit overwhelming; fortunately, visitors can choose to walk through relatively artless woods at the edge of the site to catch a glimpse of Flint's Pond.

Some of the works, like *Pine Sharks*, are site-specific installations made expressly to enhance and be enhanced by the DeCordova's landscape. The rest are either borrowed on a rotating basis from artists, dealers, and collectors or part of the museum's permanent collection. The site's atmosphere changes from year to year as large sculptures come and go.

What remains constant is the land. Much of the site is sculpture-filled lawn surrounded by white pines or oak-hickory woods. On the hillside next to the museum building is Alice's Garden, which features sculptures set among plantings of New England native perennials around a series of rough-cut granite paths, steps, and terraces—a rustic counterpoint to the elder portion of the DeCordova building, a mannerly brick castle of a summer home.

One of the most entrancing site-specific installations is on the sloping hill below the museum entrance. Ron Rudnicki's *Rain Gates* sits under tall pines. Stone steps lead from a pool to the fountain that acts as a gate of water dropping from square granite pillars. Viewers climb and descend to the pool like the water, in a forest world where liquid flows from stone.

Gropius House

68 Baker Bridge Road, Lincoln
781-259-8098 | www.historicnewengland.org/visit/homes/gropius.htm
Tours are on the hour 11:00AM–4:00PM, June 1–October 15, Wednesday–Sunday, October 16–May 31, Saturday and Sunday
Not handicap accessible
Admission is $10

The Gropius House brings its designer's sense of space and light out of the house into the wild. Close to the building, visitors enjoy intimate Japanese-influenced plantings and gravel beds. Traveling farther from the house, the plantings grow wilder and end in orchards and forest. There is no locked fence enclosing the house, shutting it off from the

world beyond. The borders between spaces are open, permeable; there is no real separation between nature and home.

The charm of the Gropius House isn't the garden *per se*; the plantings of Japanese maples, azaleas, roses, daylilies, yucca, and spring bulbs are pleasant, but not exceptional. Instead, come to the house to observe how Gropius integrated the landscape and his modernist home.

Walter Gropius, founder of the Bauhaus school of architecture, designed his family's home in 1937. Gropius and his family had fled Germany in 1934, as Hitler took control of the country. Gropius first settled in London, then moved to the United States to teach at Harvard's Graduate School of Design. When Gropius arrived in Lincoln, the site of his home was a small hill overlooking an apple orchard. Gropius had the hill leveled to build a New England–influenced jewel of modern architecture, which is now a National Historic Landmark.

Inside the Gropius House every room presents the outdoors to its onlookers; grand windows bring in light and maximize views; a screen porch and second-floor deck bring residents even closer to nature. Gropius's daughter Ati wrote, "My parents employed walls of glass to make the ever changing world of our garden a year-round extension of the living room."

Gropius sought to reproduce the historic New England landscape around his home. His retaining walls recall the remains of a stone wall found on the site, and boulders act as focal points in the landscape. He also planted New England trees: American beeches, white pines, oaks, and elms. Gropius also used vines, such as trumpet vines and Concord grapes, to connect the house with the landscape; a prominent Gropius-planted bittersweet vine still curls around a column at the rear of the house.

In 2001, Historic New England, the nonprofit which maintains the Gropius House and many other estates and gardens, embarked on a project to restore the site's landscape by replanting the orchard with Baldwin apple trees and local grasses.

Frederick Law Olmsted National Historic Site

99 Warren Street, Brookline
617-566-1689 | www.nps.gov/frla
www.friendsoffairsted.org
Call ahead
Not handicap accessible
Free

This property was the home of Boston's preeminent garden artist. Frederick Law Olmsted, designer of the finest parks in Boston's Emerald Necklace, worked and lived at this Brookline site from 1883 until his retirement in 1898. The property was designated a National Historic Site in 1979.

The site consists of Olmsted's home, Fairsted, his office building, a barn, a 1.75-acre garden Olmsted designed, and an additional five acres of woods added to the property in 1998. The site also houses archives documenting over five thousand of the Olmsted firm's landscape projects from 1883 to 1960.

The National Park Service has led a series of guided tours of Emerald Necklace parks during the site's recent renovation; check the website for details. After the renovation is completed in 2010, the site will once again allow visitors to experience the home and offices that belonged to Olmsted, the genius who designed America's most beautiful urban landscapes.

8. Gardens for Healing and Reflection

GREEN LANDSCAPES HEAL THE SOUL. BOSTONIANS HAVE BEEN creating garden sanctuaries to soothe grief and sickness since the Mount Auburn Cemetery opened in 1831. Today, cancer patients, hospitalized children, and mourners can all find respite in healing gardens at Massachusetts General Hospital, Children's Hospital, and Virginia Thurston Healing Garden, and anyone can visit the green space cemetery gardens that recall the Hub's gardening heritage.

PAGES 108–111, MOUNT AUBURN CEMETERY.

Mount Auburn Cemetery

580 Mount Auburn Street, Cambridge
617-547-7105 | www.mountauburn.org
Open September–April, 8:00AM–5:00PM;
May–August, 8:00AM–7:00PM
Handicap accessible
Free

Mount Auburn Cemetery is a grand place. Five thousand stately trees soar over one hundred and seventy-five acres of wooded paths, ponds, and hills—dwarfed only by the Washington Tower, where thousands of visitors admire the panoramic view each year. The first rural cemetery in the United States, Mount Auburn is a park, a memorial garden, a birdwatcher's paradise, and the final home of hundreds of notable Bostonians, including visionary Buckminster Fuller, novelist Bernard Malamud, poets Amy Lowell and Henry Wadsworth Longfellow, and founder of the Christian Science movement Mary Baker Eddy. Maps to popular grave sites are available at the entrance.

By the early nineteenth century, Boston's urban burying grounds were filling up. Crowded Boston cemeteries forced multiple bodies to be interred in a single grave. In the winter, when the ground was frozen and hard to dig, graves were left open until five or six bodies could be found to fill them. Editor Joseph T. Buckingham asked in the pages of the *New England Galaxy*, "Who would wish to be buried in a close city and a crowded graveyard, to be deranged and knocked about, separated and disjointed, long before the last trumpet sounds? Would we not rather lie serenely where the pure breeze rustles the honeysuckles and the field flowers, the long grass and the drooping willow, which cover and hang over our graves?"

Mount Auburn Cemetery was Boston's answer to these pleas—and a desire for privacy. The cemetery was laid out in large family plots to ensure that strangers' bones would not be commingled. Today, visitors can still see the walls and fences surrounding the earlier plots, transforming common ground into private homes for the dead.

The cemetery was established in 1831, and the landscaping and plantings were planned by Henry A. S. Dearborn, first president of the Massachusetts Horticultural Society who would go on to found Forest Hills Cemetery as well. Dearborn looked to Paris's Père Lachaise cemetery and English landscape design for inspiration. Instead of creating great lawns with carefully placed individual specimen trees, Dearborn sought to design a picturesque landscape that would appear to be established by nature itself, not through careful formal trimming and planting. The cemetery was an immediate success and became a popular destination for sightseers thrilled by the graceful, melancholic plantings shading serene graves.

Dearborn also promoted the cemetery as a laboratory for experimental horticulture, a place to grow new plants that might benefit the American economy. Today, Mount Auburn boasts over six hundred and thirty species of mature trees, including stately copper beeches and graceful willows, as well as formal ornamental gardens and native wildflower meadows.

Avian travelers also enjoy this green urban oasis with plenty of fresh-water ponds. Over two hundred and fifteen species of birds have been spotted here, and recent sightings are posted at the entrance. If you are seeking solitary solace, avoid Mount Auburn in the early mornings during the May warbler migrations, when dozens of enthusiasts with spotting scopes and binoculars swarm the place.

Forest Hills Cemetery

95 Forest Hills Avenue, Boston
617-524-0128 | www.foresthillstrust.org
Open all year, 8:30AM–dusk
Some areas handicap accessible
Free

Forest Hills was created as a place for healing. Victorian Bostonians believed that a beautiful landscape could renew and revive mourners and that death was not a time of torment or judgment, but eternal rest. Henry A. S. Dearborn's 1848 design for this garden cemetery reflects these ideas—that a park could be designed to show grieving visitors that there is still beauty and order in the world.

Dearborn was one of the first designers to plan parks around Romantic theories of landscape design, which celebrated direct contact with untamed nature—or at a minimum, nature that was carefully maintained not to appear manicured and orderly. Instead of straight roads and carefully clipped hedges, curving paths, small groves of trees, and ponds were the order of the day.

Built thirty years before the Emerald Necklace, Forest Hills Cemetery is a sprawling 250-acre monument to the idea that a well-crafted landscape could soothe troubled souls. This grand estate, along with Mount Auburn Cemetery, not only relieved

FOREST HILLS CEMETERY.

overcrowded city cemeteries but also provided a new type of park for urban visitors: a natural landscape with woods and hills and ponds and winding paths among the graves.

Fortunately for Dearborn, the Forest Hills site possessed an intriguingly varied landscape, including dramatic outcroppings of conglomerate rock known as Roxbury puddingstone, woods, and farmland. Dearborn's sympathy did not extend to the local flora, which was cleared before planting began, but he did install thousands of native and exotic specimens. Today, the majority of the canopy consists of sugar maples, red oaks, white pines, and Canadian hemlocks, but there are also specimen trees and a weeping beech over one hundred and twenty years old.

Over one hundred thousand people are buried in Forest Hills, including abolitionists, playwright Eugene O'Neill, and Boston Celtics player Reggie Lewis. However, unlike other rural cemeteries, which catered to wealthy patrons, Forest Hills was begun as a municipal cemetery and had a "potters' field" for the poor as well as lavish sites for the wealthy. Different ethnic groups have buried their dead here over the years, including Germans, Irish, Greeks, and Italians; today, Chinese and Haitian families occupy many plots—a historical cross-section of the people of Boston.

The cemetery hosts annual public rituals to honor these dead. The July Lantern Festival draws thousands of attendees, who float paper lanterns on Lake Hibiscus with messages for people who have died. November brings the Day of the Dead, a traditional Mexican festival where families bring offerings to their ancestors' graves. The cemetery also sponsors readings, including visits to the grave sites of cemetery residents such as poets e. e. cummings and Anne Sexton.

Victorian Bostonians would spend the day at Forest Hills, picnicking and strolling through the pleasant landscape and sentimental monuments. Today's visitors too can contemplate how the varied lives of Boston's past were lived and celebrated while strolling through cool pine groves and quiet lawns.

Howard Ulfelder MD Healing Garden

Massachusetts General Hospital (Charles Street entrance), Yawkey Center, Eighth Floor
617-726-2000 | www.massgeneral.org; Search: Howard Ulfelder Garden
Open all year, Monday–Friday, except holidays, 8:00AM–5:00PM
Handicap accessible
Free to Cancer Center patients, their families, and staff; others should call before visiting

This rooftop garden overlooking the Charles River could have been a simple deck with planters full of petunias and it would have been spectacular. Instead, this 6,400-square-foot garden—designed to serve patients at Massachusetts General Hospital's cancer treatment centers—is a gentle place, an Asian-inspired respite full of warm wood, gray stone, and carefully harmonized plantings. It is also a green roof, with several inches of soil storing stormwater and providing extra insulation.

Visitors enter the garden through a small glass pavilion. There are lounge chairs here, and potted ferns and orchids allow visitors some quiet green space no matter what the weather. A sign invites passers-by to hold unique stones from a pot during their stay in the garden, and a guest book invites visitors to record their reflections. In the first three years since its 2005 opening, the garden's visitors filled more than thirty books.

Rob Adams, the Halvorson Design Partnership landscape architect who designed the garden, took great care to create a garden to meet cancer patients' needs. The garden is high enough above street level that the place is quiet. A small fountain trickles over a black stone basin in summer months, lending the garden soothing sounds. There are no fragrant flowers that might nauseate a chemotherapy patient, but there is plenty of shade for light-sensitive skin. The garden features ornamental paperbark maples, Japanese maples, ornamental grasses, hostas, oakleaf hydrangeas, and highbush blueberries; it is simple without seeming austere. A central lawn gives a sense of space, while perimeter plantings continue to the edge of the site, making the garden feel like it continues right on through the transparent fence into the city air.

PROUTY TERRACE AND GARDEN.

Prouty Terrace and Garden/ Berenberg Garden

Children's Hospital, 300 Longwood Avenue, Boston
617-355-6000 | www.childrenshospital.org
Berenberg Garden open 6:00AM–9:00PM; Prouty Terrace open twenty-four hours
Handicap accessible
Free

It's a scene from a story book: walk down the right corridor at Children's Hospital and you'll suddenly wander into a sunny garden with bright flowers and animals. The animals are statues, and the broad lawn sports Keep off the Grass signs, but the place offers relief to sick children, their families, and hospital workers looking for a pleasant respite.

The Prouty Memorial Garden was built in 1956 from an Olmsted Brothers design. Modeled after the garden at New York City's original Museum of Modern Art, the garden has three sections. The largest part of the garden is an oval lawn bordered by an asphalt walkway suitable for wheelchairs. At one end of the lawn, three fish statues spit into a circular fountain. A few trees shade the walkway. The gardens around the walkway are planted with a variety of shrubs—rhododendrons, andromeda, yews—English ivy, and dollops of gaudy impatiens and other annuals. But the real attraction is the statues. Every few feet, there's another animal hidden in the bushes: a cat, a bear, an owl, a toad. A little stone rabbit huddles on the lawn, a mother bird tends to her nestlings, and a miniature St. Francis of Assisi pets a fox.

A smaller lawn to the rear features a grand dawn redwood (*Metasequoia glyptostroboides*) tree and a perennial flower bed. The garden also features a stone patio with tables and umbrellas for dining al fresco.

Straight down the corridor from the main Prouty Garden entrance is the tiny Berenberg Garden. A pocket of green with a bubbling fountain, this shady garden features stone paving and an intriguing foliage texture combination of weeping evergreens, ferns, rhododendrons, creeping juniper, and azaleas. The green palette contrasts well with russet window sills and earth-toned walls. There are no Keep off the Grass signs here (there's no grass), and children are free to play in the low stone fountain as much as they please.

Virginia Thurston Healing Garden

145 Bolton Road, Harvard
978-456-3532 | www.healinggarden.net
Open Monday–Friday, 9:00AM–5:00PM
Garden access involves travel over uneven and sloping ground; gardens can be viewed from handicap-accessible cottage
Free

Listen: the air is still. Wind chimes ring sweetly and far away a horse neighs. This eight-acre garden under towering pine trees is a place for women with breast cancer and their loved ones to sit and reflect on nature, change, and time.

Virginia Thurston had worked on her beloved garden for decades before she was diagnosed with metastatic breast cancer in 1993. She found solace in her green world and built a small garden especially for meditation. After her death in 1999, her husband, Bill, decided to open his wife's gardens to the public and renovate a cottage on the property "to provide a healing environment with no financial barriers to those experiencing breast cancer." Today, the Virginia Thurston Healing Garden offers psychological and physical support—in the cottage on-site and the garden itself—to women with breast cancer.

The path to the garden from the right-side parking lot winds through white pine woods to a grassy slope, a sort of forest oasis. The hillside lawn is dotted with islands of trees surrounded by perennial flowers. One long bed is devoted to specimen daylilies, while others feature grand old hydrangeas, andromedas, or evergreens. More evergreens and a Japanese maple frame a gazebo. At the bottom of the slope, a pair of metal water birds stoops over a small woodland pond and rocky fountain. Koi carp swim in the dark water. The garden is surrounded by woods. There are no other buildings, no streets, no places to go here; it's just the garden and the forest and the sun.

Entering the garden from the left-side parking lot brings visitors to the meditation garden, a small fenced plot recalling Japanese landscape design. A rustic trellis is modeled after traditional Japanese torii gates. Inside, there is a round stone bench below a tree and a stone Buddha.

Women who cannot tour the grounds can see the gardens from large windows in Estelle's Cottage, the healing center named for Bill's mother. His wife's gentle spirit lives on in the land she loved.

9.   Green Buildings from Top to Bottom

A BOOK ON GREEN SPACES WOULD NOT BE COMPLETE WITHOUT a chapter on the spaces where Bostonians spend most of their time: buildings. On Boston's buildings, green roof gardens range from plots of sedums at Harvard's 29 Garden Street complex and at the Children's Museum to rooftop landscapes with trees and perennials at the Boston World Trade Center. Down below, the Stata Center features an innovative garden for retaining and treating stormwater and wastewater.

In Boston, the most important thing green roofs do is reduce stormwater runoff. Once upon a time, this city was covered with forests and meadows. Rain water would fall to the ground, soak into the soil, then gradually flow into streams and rivers. Three hundred years of development have left very little open soil in Boston. Today, instead of taking up rain like a sponge, Boston sheds water like a dinner plate. Water rushes off roofs and streets, overwhelming storm drains and flushing motor oil, grease, sand, and other pollutants straight into the Charles and Mystic Rivers and Boston Harbor.

Like the fields and forests of yesteryear, soil and plant roots on the green roofs of today slow down the flow of water. Some of that water is taken up by plants; some of it is released via evaporation from the leaves and soil; and some of it simply trickles away gradually and gently. The soil and plants also help insulate the building below, reducing heating and cooling costs, and make the local area cooler by allowing water to evaporate from leaves. All these green roof features reduce strain on the city's health.

Apart from their functions, green roofs can be beautiful. Post Office Square (chapter 5), the Ulfelder Healing Garden (chapter 8), and 29 Garden Street have all won international acclaim for their gracious design—and it's hard to match the view from an open roof.

LEFT: RAY AND MARIA STATA CENTER BIOFILTRATION SWALE/GREEN ROOF.

West Podium Park (Boston World Trade Center)

Seaport Boulevard by World Trade Center
Avenue/B Street, Boston
www.seaportboston.com
Open all year
Handicap accessible via elevator
Free

From the surface streets, this small park is invisible. All you can see from Seaport Boulevard is a distant wisp of a tree and two long parallel staircases separated by a gigantic metal mesh sea serpent. Climb the stairs to arrive at a garden terrace with fourteen thousand square feet of trees, shrubs, and perennial plantings. Still, half the plantings on the site can't be seen from the garden. Another fourteen thousand square feet of roof above the garden are covered with flowering sedums.

Pressley Associates designed this award-winning green roof atop a Roofscapes Inc. engineering scheme. The soils range from five inches to three feet deep. The upper roof is covered with a pre-grown sedum mat, which was rolled up, like sod, at the nursery, then delivered and installed on-site. They are not irrigated; they simply sit and grow in harborside wind and sun. The sedums and the roof should be able to withstand 94 mph winds without damage.

The lower roof contains fifty-five varieties of trees and perennials, including Japanese zelkova trees, river birch, and oakleaf hydrangeas. The design emphasizes green textures more than ornamental flowers. Evergreen shrubs make the place look green in Boston's grayer months. A covered walkway with benches curls around the garden; there are sedums on that roof too.

West Podium Park is a welcome oasis in a well-paved part of Boston. When you are ready to descend, stroll up the street to visit Eastport Park (chapter 7) and South Boston Maritime Park (chapter 7).

Boston Children's Museum

300 Congress Street, Boston
617-426-6500 | www.bostonkids.org
Museum open daily, 10:00AM–5:00PM; Fridays, 10:00AM–9:00PM
Handicap accessible
Museum admission is $12 for adults; $9 for children (1–15) and seniors; free for children under one; $1 on Fridays, 5:00PM–9:00PM

There's enough shouting and scurrying and fun to be had that you won't notice the Boston Children's Museum's green roof if you're not looking—but if

WEST PODIUM PARK.

you do look out the upper floor windows toward Boston, you will find sixty-four hundred square feet of sedums making the world a little greener. During the Children's Museum's 2007 renovation, children and grown-ups helped prepare the soil and plant the roof.

The Boston Children's Museum lies along Fort Point Channel, an inlet of the Boston Harbor. Stormwater runoff from buildings is a major environmental concern for the site because it pollutes harbor waters. The green roof is part of the museum's plan to trap and filter stormwater runoff. Water draining from the green roof is stored in a twenty-thousand-gallon tank and later used to flush toilets and water plantings on the plaza. The museum estimates that the green roof system reduces runoff by 75 percent.

The plantings are sedums; there aren't too many plants that will survive without irrigation in the four inches of soil that the museum placed on its rooftop.

However plain the roof may appear, it represents a healthier ecosystem and is worth a look. For information about the garden on the Boston Children's Museum Plaza, see chapter 13.

4 Cambridge Center

4 Cambridge Center (Kendall Square), parking garage roof
617-523-8000
Open year-round, dawn to dusk
Accessible via elevator
Free

The rooftop garden at 4 Cambridge Center gives new meaning to the phrase office park. This football-field-sized flower-filled retreat sits high on top of a six-story parking garage right smack in the middle of Kendall Square, Cambridge's technology hub. High-rise office buildings lurk just beyond the lilies and roses, the birches and crabapples. It's a fine place to have lunch—perhaps take-out from the food court on the ground floor.

The current design is actually the second green roof on the site. In the 1980s, a topiary maze of planters full of junipers and annuals was arranged on a bed of gravel on the site. That first garden won praise as a modernist landscape; one design student even wrote a dissertation on it. Though striking when viewed from above in the two adjacent office buildings and the Kendall Square Marriott, that garden attracted few visitors; there was no shade for summer heat, and it was not handicap accessible.

Today's garden features warm brick-colored paths, patches of lawn, carefully placed trees, and plenty of flowers. When the site was renovated in 2001, designer Richard Kattman had a crew install roses, daylilies, peonies, iris, and phlox, and there are spring bulbs and seasonal plantings of annuals as well. There are benches for lounging, and a few odd little granite pillars pop up next to the path. It's a nice place to stop after viewing the more challenging designs at the Ray and Maria Stata Center across the street.

Ray and Maria Stata Center Biofiltration Swale / Green Roof

20 Vassar Street (between Buildings 56 and 57), behind Stata Center, Cambridge
http://web.mit.edu; Search: Stata Center Biofiltration
Open all year
Handicap accessible
Free

Behind the Massachusetts Institute of Technology (MIT) Stata Center (known variously as "architect Frank Gehry's masterpiece" or "that pile of tin cans on Vassar Street") are two willow trees and a river of stones between banks of green plants. During rainstorms, this dry bed becomes a real river—twice: once when the rain flows down through the garden into a fifty-thousand-gallon cistern and again when the sun comes out and a solar-powered pump brings water back to the surface to nourish the plants. This marvel of biological engineering makes the campus greener and the Charles River cleaner.

This garden is called a biofiltration swale; it's a swale (a low area) that uses plants (biology) to filter water. About half the rainwater that falls on the Stata Center is piped to this swale from roof drains. The plants' thirsty roots and the sticky soil hold enormous amounts of water and also trap oil, grease, and small particles that would otherwise clog storm drains and pollute the Charles River. The water that makes it through the soil travels to the underground cistern. After the storm ends, some of the water is slowly released to the city's storm sewers; some of it is pumped back to the Stata Center to be used to flush toilets; and some of it is used to irrigate the garden on sunny days. Altogether, MIT estimates that this biofiltration system decreases

the flow of water at a storm's peak by 50 percent and reduces the suspended particles in stormwater by 80 percent.

If you happen to stop by the Stata Center on a sunny day, you can admire native New England plants instead of filtering systems. The swale and neighboring spaces display twenty-four species, including inkberry hollies, red maples, serviceberries, sweet fern, bearberry, wintergreen, blue flag iris, cardinal flower, and decidedly non-native astilbes.

A few steps away, on the Stata Center's first-floor balcony, is a 12,000-square-foot green roof. The soil depth here, from eighteen inches to four feet, allowed the designers to plant white pines, birches, and sugar maples as well as lawn. Two more small green roof areas can be found on upper floors.

MIT has published a map of campus gardens. Most of them aren't as large or extensively engineered as the Stata Center, but they make for a pleasant visit. Download the map at web.mit.edu/facilities/environmental/gardens/gardens.html.

out neighboring buildings. It's a stunning piece of contemporary landscape design and deserves its 2007 Honor Award from the American Society of Landscape Architects.

When Harvard University renovated its graduate student residences at 29 Garden Street from 1999 to 2004, the architects at Jonathan Levi Associates saw that all the apartments looked over a 10,000-square-foot parking garage roof. Determined to use that space, the architects put down four inches of soil across the center of the space and up to three feet in planters around the roof's borders. The shallow soil and Boston's wildly fluctuating temperatures limited the selection of plants to sedums—which landscape architects at Richard Burck Associates used to create a vibrant, beautiful landscape.

Harvard's campus is host to several other less famous green roofs; for a listing, see www.greencampus.harvard.edu.

29 Garden Street

29 Garden Street, Cambridge
Open all year
Handicap accessible
Free

The first thing you notice at 29 Garden Street is the colors. The second-floor plaza glows in alternating strips of deep red and lime green sedums and paved walkways. Then the texture appears—the sedums' irregular heights and leaves make subtle patterns, like a piece of New England tundra. A wooden walkway arcs across the sedums to a circular bench; across the plaza, planters with witch hazel trees and evergreen shrubs screen

CitySprouts Gardens

Locations in Cambridge
617-876-2436 | citysprouts.org
Check website for weekly open times and locations
Handicap accessible; call about specific sites
Free

If you visit a CitySprouts garden, don't expect to just sit back and linger by the flowers. At any minute, you might be asked to help water the insect-eating pitcher plants in a bog garden, plant the potato crops, or measure if the scarlet runner bean vines are taller than the Kentucky Wonders—that is, if the young gardeners don't get there first.

To promote good health and environmental stewardship, CitySprouts has been creating learning gardens at Cambridge public schools since 1999. With the help of CitySprouts coordinators, students at ten schools nurture small and large gardens full of healthy food and beautiful blooms. The gardens grow an amazing variety of plants in small spaces: lacy dill plants peek out behind the corn stalks and bountiful beans cascade over walls. Everywhere, there are hints of what the students are learning. There are signs describing the plants in English and Spanish, rain gauges and thermometers to track the weather, even a garden with a different plant for each letter. (X is for *Xanthorhiza,* or yellowroot, in case you were wondering.)

CitySprouts sponsors weekly garden drop-ins. During drop-ins, visitors can either work in the garden or learn about how to grow and eat the plants; students may press apple cider from fruit grown in their schoolyard, grind their grown wheat into flour, or cook up stir-fries from greens and garlic they harvest themselves.

All the CitySprouts schools thrive under the children's careful tending, but the Morse School and Amigos/Martin Luther King School gardens are two of the oldest and largest gardens. The expansive Morse School garden is visible from the street. With dozens of plantings and a mature apple tree, it's a small farm a block from the Charles River. The Amigos/Martin Luther King School garden on Putnam Avenue can be tricky for visitors to find—it can only be entered through a downstairs cafeteria— but features elegant, towering grape trellises and carefully designed beds and hardscape. A small pond and a great painted compass rose brighten a once-desolate concrete courtyard there.

Clark-Cooper Community Garden

Boston Nature Center and Wildlife Sanctuary, 500 Walk Hill Street, Mattapan
617-983-8500 | www.massaudubon.org; Search: Boston Nature Center
Open all year
Paths within the garden are gravel, dirt, or mulch-covered
Free

It's a grand scene: a vast field of 276 sunny garden plots surrounded by a wooden fence and lush trees. The Clark-Cooper Community Garden is one of the oldest and largest community gardens in Boston, and its gardeners have built an exceptional site. The grounds feature gravel paths, a brick building with a bathroom, a handsome sign—and yards and yards of tomatoes, collard greens, and anything else its gardeners care to grow. The borders of the garden are lined with one hundred fruit trees and bushes planted by Earthworks Boston in 1998 and 1999, including apple, pear, plum, cherry, pawpaw, Juneberry, hazelnut, and pecan trees, a

lone chestnut, and raspberry, blueberry, currant, and elderberry bushes.

Local residents founded the garden in 1969 on what was once the west campus of the Boston State Hospital. After the hospital closed in 1979, the hospital grounds were neglected for almost two decades. In 1996, the Massachusetts Audubon Society established the Boston Nature Center (chapter 6) on the sixty-seven-acre site. While Audubon owns the property, the gardens are managed by a separate group, Clark-Cooper Community Garden Incorporated. Audubon raised money to redesign the garden in 1999, changing the location of the garden, placing plots closer together than the community gardeners had previously laid them out, and providing water faucets and a tool storage shed. The gardens continue to be popular, productive, and beautiful.

FENWAY VICTORY GARDENS.

Fenway Victory Gardens

Boylston Street, Park Drive, and the Fenway
(Back Bay Fens), Boston
617-267-6650 | fenwayvictorygardens.com
Open all year
Fens paths are paved; paths within Victory
Gardens may be gravel, dirt, or mulch-covered
Free

Keep walking. That's the only way you're going to get to see the Fenway Victory Gardens' five hundred whimsical, lovely, productive plots. This great-granddaddy of all community gardens has been growing for over sixty years. Spanning seven acres, it features plots fifteen feet by twenty feet, big enough to encourage amateur landscapers to create entire backyards on the site. Many gardeners have been improving their sites for decades. You'll find elaborate arbors and roses, lilacs and lilies, Japanese gardens with raked stones and small evergreens, paved paths and peach trees, sunflowers and gorgeous tomatoes and enormous kale; just keep walking.

The Fenway Victory Gardens, founded in 1942, is one of the last remaining public Victory Gardens, plots that were farmed in urban areas during World War II to combat food shortages. Officially, they're the Richard D. Parker Memorial Victory Gardens, named for a member of the original organizing committee who defended the gardens from being converted to other uses over the years.

Today, the gardens are known for their sheer size and variety, and their parties. The yearly fall Fens Fest features live music and awards in categories like Best Secret Garden, Wildlife Friendly Garden, and Best Shrubbery.

Christian Herter Community Garden / Charles River Community Garden

Charles River Reservation near the Public Theater, 1155 Soldiers Field Road (Herter), and the Northeastern University Boat House, 1450 Soldiers Field Road (Charles River), Brighton
www.bostonnatural.org/cgFind.htm
Open all year
Charles River Reservation is handicap accessible; garden access requires travel across lawn
Free

These two community gardens are located less than half a mile apart along the shores of the Charles River, making for a pleasant stroll. The Herter Garden features a working windmill that pumps water from the Charles River to irrigate the gardens. David

Carlson's plot at the Charles River garden has won multiple Mayor's Garden Contest awards. There's ample parking at the Public Theater lot.

Gardens for Charlestown

Main and Bunker Hill Streets (near Sullivan Square), Charlestown
www.charlestownonline.net/gardens.htm
Open daily, dawn to dusk
Paths within gardens are grassy or mulch-covered
Free

This venerable sixty-three-plot community garden has been cultivated since 1976. The one-block site is meticulously organized and maintained and is a stark contrast to the neighborhood density and busy highways nearby. The Charlestown gardens concentrate on annual and perennial flowers, although there are also plenty of vegetables and a small Japanese-styled plot here too. Several mature fruit trees grow along the street-side fences.

The Food Project Gardens

Langdon and George Streets, Roxbury; West Cottage Street by Brook Avenue, Dorchester; Albion Street, Boston; Boston Medical Center, One Boston Medical Center Place, Boston
617-442-1322 | www.thefoodproject.org
See website for details on market season

GARDENS FOR CHARLESTOWN.

The Food Project gardens are not just pleasant, orderly places to see corn and eggplant growing on city lots. They share a serious mission to provide fresh, affordable local produce to low-income neighborhood residents who have limited access to supermarkets. Producing fifteen thousand to eighteen thousand pounds of fresh vegetables a year, the Food Project plots supply vegetables to the Dudley Town Commons farmers' markets as well as to local nonprofits like Rosie's Place and Community Servings. It's all part of the Food Project's goal to bring community youth and adults together to create a sustainable urban food system—and also make vacant lots more beautiful.

The Food Project began farming its first urban site at the Langdon Street garden in 1996. They added the West Cottage site in 1997 and the Albion site in 2001. All three of these urban farms required extensive work—removing trash, placing boulders and fences to keep cars from parking on-site, and adding tons of soil and compost to reduce soil lead levels. Since the gardens were created, the Food Project has practiced preserving the soil's fertility by sustainable agriculture methods, including hand tilling, sowing cover crops, rotating crops, and adding compost to the soil. Some of the compost is made on-site, although production is limited by the gardens' area and neighbors' sense of aesthetics. You can visit ten-foot-long bins at the West Cottage Street site.

Today, these sites are model urban farms. All three feature a variety of food crops and cheerful annual flowers, including marigolds, zinnias, and sunflowers, neatly sown in rows and carefully

THE FOOD PROJECT GARDENS

tended. The largest garden is the 1.4-acre farm on West Cottage Street, which features brightly colored murals on its storage sheds at the rear of the site.

Additionally, The Food Project farms six thousand square feet atop a parking garage at the Boston Medical Center, harvesting upwards of twenty-five hundred pounds of produce a year. The Food Project also farms plots in Lincoln and at Long Hill in Beverly.

ReVision House Urban Farm

38 Fabyan Street, Dorchester
617-822-FARM (3276)
www.vpi.org/Re-VisionFarm
Farm stand open Thursday afternoons; call for hours

On a small lot in Dorchester, women are growing food—and gaining new lives. On average, ReVision House shelters twenty-two homeless women with children for stays ranging from six to eighteen months. The ReVision House Urban Farm's Fabyan Street plots are home to a fence painted with murals, a greenhouse, and hundreds of orderly organically grown plants: squash, collards, tomatoes, zinnias, eggplant, cucumbers, sweet potatoes, callaloo,

REVISION HOUSE URBAN FARM.

and dozens of others. These two plots and a third ReVision House site make up a little over an acre of land; in 2007, ReVision's residents raised more than fifty-three hundred pounds of food.

ReVision House provides its residents with shelter and a variety of programs, including job training. The urban farm is part of that training. ReVision residents take on many farm tasks and gain experience in small-scale farming, greenhouse management, marketing, and community outreach. Neighborhood residents gain fresh, nutritious, affordable food. Half the harvest goes to feed ReVision house residents; the rest is distributed through the farm stand, farmers' markets, and a joint CSA with Drumlin Farm of Lincoln.

ReVision House runs a farm stand on the site on Thursday afternoons during the growing season. During the gray winter months, customers can pre-order seedlings that the ReVision residents grow in the on-site greenhouse, including vegetables, herbs, annual flowers, and a dozen varieties of tomatoes. Orders are generally due in early February for pick-up in April or May.

Newton Community Farm

303 Nahanton Street, Newton
617-916-9655
www.newtoncommunityfarm.org/index.htm
Open all year
Paths within the farm may be gravel, dirt, or mulch-covered
Free

It's a small place with a big idea. The 2.25-acre Newton Community Farm, owned by the city of Newton, is the last operating farm in town. Newton is known for its safe streets and high-flying schools and has had much more success building houses than growing crops over the decades since World War II. Thanks to prescient planning by Newton's citizens, today the site has a farmhouse, a barn, and a shed instead of two acres of condos.

This site has been farmed continuously for more than three hundred years The Angino family moved to the property in 1917. By 2005, the last Angino farmer was ready to retire. Public support and new money from Newton's adoption of the Community Preservation Act allowed the city to buy the land before it fell into developers' hands.

Today, the nonprofit Newton Community Farm Inc. (NCF) tills the land rent-free but gets no farming assistance from the city. NCF hires a farm manager to oversee the farm and coordinate volunteers and students who come to work the land.

The NCF uses many low-impact agricultural techniques to coax a hefty load of produce from the soil. The farm is not certified organic, but uses organic methods to maintain plant health—reduced tilling, compost, and "green manure" crops. No herbicides or synthetic fertilizers are used on the farm.

The farm is developing several beds using bio-intensive methods for sustainably increasing plant productivity. The farm is also creating permaculture plots, where mixes of plants should sustain themselves with little maintenance (apart from harvesting!) for years.

The NCF sponsors various programs, from classes in making jelly to workshops on composting with worms. Alert Newton residents can enroll in the Community Supported Agriculture (CSA) produce subscription program, which is limited to seventy-five members; the shares tend to sell out before out-of-towners are allowed to apply for them.

NEWTON COMMUNITY FARM.

Earthworks Boston

If you see a perfect Roxbury russet apple on a tree along a Boston street, look for an Earthworks sign. Chances are that Earthworks planted it, and it's there for the picking—just one of the hundreds of fruit-bearing trees, shrubs, and vines Earthworks has installed in neighborhoods around town. Thanks to Earthworks, forty-seven sites in Boston, Cambridge, Somerville, and Brookline are growing apples, pears, cherries, plums, mulberries, persimmons, pecans, and hazelnuts as well as Juneberries, raspberries, strawberries, grapes, and kiwis.

Founded in 1989, Earthworks seeks to create urban orchards, restore urban wilds, and provide outdoor classrooms to urban schools. By helping urban residents in underserved communities grow fruit and plant trees, Earthworks helps to strengthen residents' ties to nature—and to each other.

One site that Earthworks has been working hard to tame is the McLaughlin Woods (Fisher Avenue between Bucknam Street and Parker Street, Jamaica Plain). In the eighteenth century, the hill was known as the Parker Farm. Parker, an apple devotee, produced hard cider and was killed when a barrel of his liquor fell on him. The land is currently owned by New England Baptist Hospital, but a conservation restriction legally bars any development on the site.

In 1992, Earthworks planted nut trees on the site; in the late 1990s, that small orchard was expanded with fifty apple, pear, plum, apricot, persimmon, hazelnut, chestnut, and Juneberry trees. The apples and pears are heirloom varieties dating from Boston's eighteenth-century orchards. Earthworks has also removed large quantities of invasive plants and installed hundreds of native trees and shrubs, including gray dogwoods, buttonbush, red chokecherries, paper birches, American beeches, hickories, and sugar maples.

Botanical detectives, this is your park. All those trees are visible in the forest—if you can find them. The trees are healthy, but unlabeled, and scattered through the site. The slopes along Fisher Avenue appear to be an overgrown green jumble to casual visitors—but astute pomologists can spot apple trees that may be the descendants of an eighteenth-century orchard. If you wish to search for the specimens on the McLaughlin site, search carefully, and don't forget to look at your feet; once you leave the paved paths, you'll find plenty of poison ivy.

Other visitors will enjoy the eleven-acre site's playground, stone block seats, and an open hilltop with distant views of Boston Harbor.

To find out how to help make Boston greener (and tastier), visit www.earthworksboston.org.

Elm Bank

Massachusetts Horticultural Society, Elm Bank
Reservation, 900 Washington Street (Route 16),
Wellesley
617-933-4900 | www.masshort.org
Open daily, 8:00AM–dusk
Handicap accessible
Free

Elm Bank isn't a botanical garden. It's seven gardens showcasing different types of landscape design and popular plant cultivars: the New England Trial Garden, the Bressingham Garden, the Italianate Garden, the Jim Crockett Memorial Garden, the New England Daylily Society Garden, the Alan Payton Rhododendron Display Garden, and Weezie's Garden for Children (chapter 13), as well as smaller displays of ornamental grasses and herbs on the grounds. Keeping track of all these gardens can be a bit confusing because there isn't much signage at Elm Bank. Ask for assistance at Flora, the gift shop at the site's entrance.

The Massachusetts Horticultural Society gained their first open-air headquarters here in 1996; previously, the society had been housed in various buildings in Boston. The society's first garden on the site, the New England Trial Garden, was established that same year. A joint venture of Mass Hort, the University of Massachusetts, and the Massachusetts Flower Growers' Association, the Trial Garden is a series of rectangular flower beds, with a few large stone-faced raised beds in the center. There are plenty of petunias, impatiens, ageratum, and other familiar flowers.

Visitors who prefer a less orderly landscape will appreciate the Bressingham Garden, created by British garden designer Adrian Bloom. With the help of nearly two hundred volunteers who had come to work with the garden master, Bloom installed this one-acre garden on what was once grassy lawn in 2007. It's a complex landscape of perennials, trees, and shrubs, and some of the combinations of hot-colored summer-blooming perennials are astonishingly vibrant. Everywhere there is attention to form, to texture, and to creating a landscape for all four seasons. It will be interesting to see the garden develop as the trees and shrubs mature; a complete plant list is available at the Mass Hort website.

The Italianate Garden in front of the Elm Bank neo-Georgian manor house has been restored in accordance with a 1926 plan for the site by the Olmsted Brothers firm. This formal garden consists of a level lawn split by a long central stonedust path from the garden's entrance to the front door of the house. A large white fountain surrounded by a circular walk dominates the center of the site, and specimen trees are scattered about; specimens include a Camperdown elm and a weeping larch. The paths are lined with annual flowers in deep reds and purple, and the entire grand rectangle is enclosed in a high purple beech hedge. The effect is elegant.

The Jim Crockett Memorial Garden is dedicated to the long-term host of the television show *The Victory Garden*. This small plot features poppies from *The Victory Garden*'s colony and the *Boltonia asteroides* cultivar 'Jim Crockett', as well as benches for fatigued visitors.

The New England Daylily Society Garden displays more than six hundred *Hemerocallis* cultivars in a very simple fashion: they're lined up in two rectangular beds along a paved walkway. Some varieties date back to the sixteenth century, although these particular plants arrived at Elm Bank in 2004. This garden is at its peak in July, but visitors can find daylilies in bloom from May until frost.

Planted in 2002–2003, the Alan Payton Rhododendron Display Garden has eighty varieties of rhododendrons as well as fifteen varieties of ground covers and a few ornamental trees. The plants spread out over four plots that roughly form a trapezoid with a kidney-shaped center bed. Visit this garden in early May for peak bloom; however, observers will find flowers any time from early April through frost. A map of the garden with a plant list is available on the Mass Hort website.

If you tire of all these planned landscapes, there is relief at hand. The remaining one hundred and forty-six acres of the Elm Bank Reservation feature many forested walking trails and paths along the Charles River.

Over the past decade, the Massachusetts Horticultural Society has been suffering increasingly severe financial problems, culminating in the society calling off the 2009 New England Flower Show. This cancellation is a significant event: it marks the first break of the longest continuously running flower show in the world—one hundred and thirty-seven shows.

Alexandra Botanic Garden/ H. H. Hunnewell Arboretum

Wellesley College, Route 135, Wellesley
781-283-3094 | www.wellesley.edu/WCBG
Visitor center open daily, 8:00AM–4:00PM
Paths through gardens pass over
uneven ground, hilly terrain
Free

Wellesley College's leafy suburban campus is the home of three botanical collections: the Alexandra Botanic Garden, the H. H. Hunnewell Arboretum, and the Margaret C. Ferguson Greenhouses (chapter 12). Among the college's glacial landscape of rolling hills, forest, ponds, and streams, the Alexandra Botanic Garden and Hunnewell Arboretum feature five hundred species of trees and shrubs from fifty-three different families. It's a charming place to walk, and the college and the Wellesley College Friends of Horticulture have produced maps and other documentation of the collections; that information is available online or at the greenhouse visitor center.

The Hunnewell Arboretum takes its name from Horatio Hollis Hunnewell, a wealthy banker and ardent Wellesley supporter whose wife, Isabella Pratt Welles, lent the college her name. The arboretum features several different habitats, including forest fragments with tall native oaks and hickories, a red maple swamp, and some meadow. Visitors may especially enjoy sneaking into a hidden grotto near a planting of Japanese maples. Springtime is show time at the arboretum, when collections of rhododendrons, lilacs, and azaleas come into bloom.

The Alexandra Botanic Garden is located on the other side of a paved pathway from the arboretum. This garden was named for Alexandra Severance, who died at age six. Her mother, Mary Severance, was an 1885 Wellesley graduate. Mary and her husband, Cordenio, donated funds to start the garden in 1906. Paramecium Pond and its brook stretch through this site, which features flowering cherries and crabapples, towering oaks, Chinese cork trees, hydrangeas, hawthorns, and walnuts. There are pine groves and open meadows along the brook. Specimen trees in this area include a dawn redwood, European beeches, Japanese stewartia, and a golden larch.

The campus itself has been extensively renovated in recent years by Michael Van Valkenburgh Associates. The renovation sought to restore the campus's ecological and pedestrian functions. When Wellesley's land was assembled in 1875, the campus's founders envisioned a series of meadows, hills, and valleys linked by winding walking paths; Frederick Law Olmsted's 1902 plan for the campus endorsed the idea, as did a 1921 site plan by Frederick Law Olmsted Jr., Arthur Shurcliff, and architect Ralph Adams Cram. Unfortunately, over the twentieth century, Wellesley embraced the automobile. Olmstedian meadows were covered with parking lots, valleys were filled with contaminated construction debris, and roads overwhelmed the landscape. From 1997 to 2005, Michael Van Valkenburgh Associates drew up a new master plan for the campus and renovated thirteen and a half acres of neglected, contaminated land around what is now the Lulu Chow Wang Campus Center. A 175-car parking lot has been replaced with small hills, meadows, lawn, and a cattail-edged pond—all concealing clever topographical features that filter contaminants out of stormwater before it reaches nearby Lake Waban.

There are several more specialized gardens near the greenhouses, including a sensory garden of sweet-smelling plants, a small green roof, and a butterfly garden.

Garden in the Woods

180 Hemenway Road, Framingham
508-877-7630 | www.newfs.org
Open April 15–Labor Day, open Tuesday–Sunday and Holiday Mondays, 9:00AM–5:00PM, Thursday and Friday to 7:00PM; July 4–October 31 open Tuesday–Sunday and Holiday Mondays, 9:00AM–5:00PM. Closed November 1–April 14
Not handicap accessible; unpaved garden paths, steps, and uneven terrain
Adults, $8; seniors, $6; youths (3–18), $4; students (with student ID), $6; children under three, free; New England Wild Flower Society members, free

The New England Wild Flower Society's (NEWFS) mission is to conserve North American native plants—and the Garden in the Woods is a grand place to start appreciating them. With more than fifteen hundred native plant species on forty-five acres of woods, wetlands, and meadows, the Garden in the Woods is the largest landscaped collection of wildflowers in the Northeast. It's also a pretty, shady place to spend an afternoon. There are massive pines and oaks, brilliant plumes of black cohosh flowers, yellow lady slipper orchids, foamflowers, dogwoods, turtleheads—the grand list goes on and on. You won't find orderly beds here, NEWFS prefers a more natural look, but you will find plant labels for most of the common and curious specimens here.

The Garden in the Woods was once an estate belonging to Will Curtis, one of NEWFS's founders. He began experimenting with growing native plants on the site in the 1930s. Curtis left the property to the society in 1965. Since then, the society has faithfully cultivated the site.

The main trail is about a mile long, though visitors have the option of taking longer walks through wilder

GARDEN IN THE WOODS.

wooded areas. The trail passes through several different habitats, including a New England bog, a rocky alpine area, and a sunny, sweet-smelling meadow flush with hovering butterflies. Casual visitors and children will enjoy a lily pond, home to fish, turtles, and occasional ducks. Gardeners will appreciate the on-site nursery, where anyone can buy dozens of sturdy NEWFS-raised native plants; anyone who spends time in the wild will appreciate the ubiquitous plant labels, which allow observers the chance to finally identify that pretty little flower they saw off the trail last summer.

Remember that this is the Garden in the Woods— which means that between late May and mid-September, the site is also a Garden of Mosquitoes. Some bug repellant is available at the gift shop if you forget to pack your own.

The New England Wild Flower Society

Would you like to learn to grow lady slipper orchids? Or go on a guided tour of a bog? Perhaps you'd enjoy being part of a team of plant detectives working to find invasive plants poised to attack public lands. Whatever your pleasure, if it involves wild plants in New England, you can find it at the New England Wild Flower Society (NEWFS).

Founded in 1900 as the Society for the Protection of Native Plants, NEWFS works to conserve wild plants, from alpine flowers on Mount Washington's summit to seaside succulents. In between, the society operates ten sanctuaries for rare and endangered plants and raises more than seven hundred native plant species and cultivars for sale—seventy-five thousand plants a year.

After you visit a few NEWFS sites, you might find yourself waking up nights thinking, "Wait, was that common self-heal or skullcap?" If so, consider availing yourself of one of the NEWFS botany courses, where you will learn to confuse *Prunella vulgaris* and *Scutellaria incana* instead. NEWFS also offers classes in native plants, horticulture, and landscape design, including field trips throughout New England.

12. Green Within: Greenhouses and Courtyards

IN THE DEPTHS OF GRAY WINTER, BOSTON'S ENCLOSED GARDENS offer lush, sweet-smelling respites from the ice and cold. The Isabella Stewart Gardner Museum's courtyard garden encloses Mediterranean stone fountains and statuary along with dozens of winter-blooming jasmine trees and azaleas, while Waltham's Lyman Estate boasts gardenias and orchids. The Margaret C. Emerson Greenhouses shelter water lilies and goldfish in a small, peaceful pond. Further afield, the Tower Hill Botanic Garden's Orangerie is a gymnasium-sized atrium scented with flowers of orange trees and Persian limes.

LEFT & PAGES 146–147: ISABELLA STEWART GARDNER MUSEUM COURTYARD.
ABOVE: MARGARET C. FERGUSON GREENHOUSES.

Isabella Stewart Gardner Museum Courtyard

280 Fenway, Boston
617-566-1401 | www.gardnermuseum.org
Open Tuesday–Sunday, 11:00AM–5:00PM
Most galleries overlooking the courtyard are handicap accessible
Adults, $12; seniors, $10; college students, $5; children under 18, free. Women named Isabella admitted free with ID

This stately museum—with fine art by Titian, Rembrandt, Michelangelo, and dozens of other artists—can be a bit overwhelming. But the central courtyard is lovely enough to revive tired eyes.

Gardner was wealthy, devoted to the arts, and very particular. Her 1924 will dictated that her extensive art collection be displayed exactly as she left it—instructions ignored by burglars who made off with $300 million of art in an unsolved 1990 theft. Fortunately, the plantings were left intact.

Under a glass roof three stories above, this Mediterranean-style garden is planted with myrtle, bay, and a selection of flowers that changes six times annually (a schedule of upcoming plantings is available on the museum's website). The walls around the courtyard are modeled after a fifteenth-century Venetian palace, with tall windows and plenty of balconies all around. In April, the museum decorates second-floor balconies with nasturtium vines up to twenty feet long to commemorate Isabella Stewart Gardner's birthday; the museum cafe offers celebratory dishes made with edible nasturtium flowers. The plethora of windows and balconies is fortunate, as museum visitors are not allowed into the courtyard. Standing on those lovely balconies is as close as you're going to get to the flowers Gardner held so dear.

Gardner's garden consists of formal plantings laid out around a large central floor mosaic. Patches of grass and containers of flowers and ferns are interspersed with classical statuary. Gardner herself was an amateur horticulturist; she even raised award-winning orchids in her on-site greenhouse.

Lyman Estate Greenhouses

185 Lyman Street, Waltham
781-891-4882 | www.historicnewengland.org
Open December 15–July 15, Wednesday–Sunday, 9:30AM–4:00PM (7:00PM on Thursday); July 16–December 14, closed Sunday
Not handicap accessible (narrow passages, stairs)
Guided tours (first Wednesdays, on the hour, 11:00AM–2:00PM) are $6 for non-members; Historic New England members, free

If you've ever imagined working at a Victorian manor house as a gardener cultivating rare orchids to suit your master's exacting tastes, come visit the Lyman Estate. The oldest greenhouse there dates to 1804 and is built of brick, stucco, iron, and glass, with nary a Jiffy Pot or plastic plant marker to be seen. Instead, visitors can view camellias, orchids, bougainvillea, or 130-year-old Black Hamburg grape vines raised from cuttings from the royal greenhouses at England's Hampton Court Palace.

The Lyman greenhouses were first built to provide a Boston merchant named Thomas Lyman (1753–1839) with winter fruits and vegetables. The complex is long and narrow so that the greenhouses can be heated almost entirely by solar energy in the winter. The greenhouses face southeast; sunlight penetrates the slanted glass roof and warms the brick walls, which radiate heat at night. Daytime winter temperatures in the oldest greenhouse stay

between eighty degrees and ninety degrees. For chilly evenings, arched passages allow heat from the basement furnace to rise up to the plants.

Hundreds of tender plants enjoy this careful engineering. Three Grape Houses shelter the stately espaliered grape vines as well as dwarf citrus trees, bougainvillea vines, and smaller botanical gems. The Orchid House encloses dozens of species orchids and hybrid orchids, all lovely, some rare. Just beyond the orchids, the Camellia House features thirteen century-old trees which burst with bright red, white, and pink blooms from December through April.

Gardeners can purchase plants, books, and souvenirs at the sales greenhouse and gift shop, where you may find the resident greenhouse cat staring at the goldfish lolling in a small pond. The Lyman Estate hosts several special shows and sales of orchids, wild flowers, herbs, camellias, and other plants.

Margaret C. Ferguson Greenhouses

Wellesley College, Route 135, Wellesley
781-283-3094 | www.wellesley.edu/WCBG
Visitor center open daily, 8:00AM–4:00PM
Handicap accessible
Free

Walk into the Margaret C. Ferguson Greenhouses and enter another world—or two, or four. The greenhouses are named for Margaret C. Ferguson, a professor in Wellesley's Botany Department from 1901 to 1938 and the first woman president of the Botanical Society of America. These intimate greenhouses contain more than one thousand plants in nine different plant displays ranging from desert to tropical jungle.

Visitors enter through the Desert Plants Room, then walk through the Seasonal Display House to view a 128-year-old camellia tree, the last remaining camellia donated by the college's founder, Henry Durant. A pretty arch of trailing nasturtium vines decorates the aptly named Nasturtium Arch Room—but it's the Tropical Plant Room that impresses most visitors.

The largest of these small greenhouses, the Tropical Plant Room houses layers of verdant tropical plants from groundcovers to vines to trees. This twenty-foot-tall greenhouse harbors banana trees and coffee bushes, bromeliads, Australian tree ferns, and traveler's palms. The air is thick and moist, and the textured wall of green is a welcome sight in a New England winter.

The neighboring Subtropical Room features many familiar-looking houseplants whose ancestors once grew in mild climates. A Cryptogam Room is devoted primarily to ferns; the Begonia Room to a riot of the enormous, often pink-flowered, plants. Another room shelters pitcher plants, insectivorous plants that drown flies in pools of sticky liquid. The most peaceful place in the greenhouse is the Water Plants Room, where visitors can sit and contemplate papyrus, mangrove, and floating water lilies while a frog fountain spits water into a small koi pond.

None of the rooms are particularly large: kids could run through the place in ten minutes. But they are green when the world outside is gray, and for careful observers, treasures abound.

MARGARET C. FERGUSON GREENHOUSES.

Tower Hill Botanic Garden Orangerie

11 French Drive, Boylston
508-869-6111 | www.towerhillbg.org
Open Tuesday–Sunday, plus Monday holidays,
10:00AM–5:00PM
Handicap accessible
Adults, $10; seniors, $7; youth (6–18), $5;
Worcester members and children under six, free

Although it's an hour's drive from Boston, in the middle of February, it's worth it. The largest conservatory in the Boston area, the Tower Hill Botanic Garden Orangerie is a huge, magnificent, sweet-smelling glass-roofed greenhouse replete with banana trees, palm trees, lemons, orchids, even a Surinam powderpuff tree—and yes, oranges.

The orangerie is a single 4,000-square-foot room, about the size of a gymnasium, built to mimic eighteenth-century conservatories. A raised central roof accommodates the tallest palms, and below the orangerie's floor is a pit greenhouse—a dark area where plants are allowed to rest before the seasons when they are forced into bloom.

There are three layers of winter-blooming subtropical plants in the orangerie. At the top are soaring palms from Madagascar, Southeast Asia, and Central America. In the middle are camellias and citrus trees, including Meyer lemon, calamondin oranges, and Persian limes. These citrus trees are commonly in bud, bloom, and fruit at the same time, scenting the air and making identification easy. Below, there are bromeliads, ferns, and flowering plants, including clivias. The place is a raucous, rich tapestry of leaves, gaudy blooms, and sweet smells.

If you happen to visit Tower Hill outside of winter months, fear not! There are several other intriguing gardens on-site, including a wildlife garden, an orchard with one hundred and nineteen heirloom apple varieties, a cottage garden, and an Italianate systematic garden designed to show evolutionary relationships within plant families. If fatigue overtakes you, consider admiring the local geography instead; the on-site cafe provides distant views of Mount Wachusett.

13.   Green Play

MOST BOSTON PARKS FEATURE A PLAYGROUND. COLUMBUS PARK,
the Boston Common, and the Charles River Esplanade all have scenic
playgrounds, and generations of children have ridden on the *Make Way
for Ducklings* statues at Boston's Public Garden. However, there are three
gardens near Boston specifically designed for children: the bustling Boston
Children's Museum Plaza; the Children's Garden at the Hyde Park Branch of
the Boston Public Library; and Weezie's Garden for Children in Wellesley.

OPPOSITE: WEEZIE'S GARDEN FOR CHILDREN. ABOVE: BOSTON CHILDREN'S MUSEUM PLAZA.

Boston Children's Museum Plaza

300 Congress Street, Boston
617-426-6500 | www.bostonkids.org
Plaza open twenty-four hours. Museum
open daily, 10:00AM–5:00PM; Fridays,
10:00AM–9:00PM
Handicap accessible
Plaza is free; museum admission is $12 for adults;
$9, children (1–15) and seniors; free, children
under one; $1 on Fridays, 5:00PM–9:00PM

The actual green space here will look small to grown-ups—but it's the right size for young imaginations. There are big rocks, a little garden of native plants you can touch and smell, a crazy maze in the paving stones, and expansive views of Boston across the Fort Point Channel.

This kooky, curious plaza won a 2008 General Design Honor Award from the American Society of Landscape Architects for being "playful and daring." Michael Van Valkenburgh Associates planned this plaza as part of the Children's Museum's 2007 renovations. The firm worked with museum staff and play experts to design a space that could be used for large festivals, but also for exploratory play.

At the Congress Street end of the plaza is the forty-foot-tall Hood milk bottle, a Children's Museum icon for decades. The pavement maze is here, just the right size for running wildly on its crooked paths. A few willow trees decorate the space. Farther along the plaza are a series of ten-foot-tall marble boulders for playing peekaboo, hide-and-seek, or the ever popular run-in-circles-around-the-boulders game. At the far edge of the plaza is a small native plant garden. The path is staggered through the rectangular plot; you can't see directly ahead of you, and the plants are tall enough that children can't see over them either. For a few moments, you are surrounded by green. Several sweet fern plants line the channel side of the path; kids can run their fingers over the leaves and smell a sunny summer field in their hands. Kids who just want to keep running can continue on past the plaza on the Boston Harborwalk (chapter 2).

For more information about the Children's Museum's green roof and stormwater management system, see chapter 9.

Children's Garden, Hyde Park Branch Library

35 Harvard Avenue, Hyde Park
617-361-2524
www.bpl.org/branches/hyde.htm
Open Monday and Thursday, noon–8:00PM;
Tuesday and Wednesday, 10:00AM–6:00PM;
Friday, 9:00AM–5:00PM
Handicap accessible
Free

When children tire of stories and start to wiggle off laps, relief is at hand. This small-scale garden sits in a fenced courtyard adjoining the children's section of the Hyde Park Branch Library and is available for romping, rolling, or simply sitting in the sun.

A small patch of lawn lines one side. The rest of the plot is covered with stone paths and mulch winding around cedars, fruit trees, and boulders just tall enough for most toddlers to climb. The boulders are inscribed with verses of the poem "The End" by A. A. Milne, author of *Winnie the Pooh*. Literate children will scamper about reading the rocks: "When I was One, / I had just begun." The children's garden should encourage good reading habits—or at least close examination of boulders—for years to come.

Weezie's Garden for Children

Massachusetts Horticultural Society, Elm Bank
Reservation, 900 Washington Street (Route 16),
Wellesley
617-933-4900 | www.masshort.org
Open daily, 8:00AM–dusk
Handicap accessible
Free

You can't walk straight into Weezie's Garden: the
paths curve and spiral around dozens of places to
wander, climb, and play. Children can run in circles
around a rocky fountain, clamber up a rustic tower,
or simply sit and poke around in a sand pit under
the banana trees. There are dozens of green worlds
in this one-acre site, and kids can touch them, smell
them, and explore them freely.

The fountain, tower, and sand form the center
of the garden, and many children will be happy
to spend an afternoon digging, climbing, and
pumping water into the rocky pool. But paths also
spiral out beyond the center lawns to the edges
of the site. There, young adventurers will discover
hidden shade gardens with red maples and granite
stones, a Bamboo Garden behind an enormous
bright red rocking chair, and a Bluebird Garden
with a birdhouse and child-sized nests woven out
of branches—all ready to be stepped on, poked,
and climbed.

Bright flowers throughout the site attract bees
and butterflies and scent the air: wild native plants
echinacea and rudbeckia dominate the wing-shaped
butterfly gardens at the rear, while domesticates
such as petunias and dahlias bloom at the entrance.
The soft-leaved plant lamb's ear awaits a child's
touch, as do the rotating flowers of the obedient
plants (*Physostegia virginiana*).

If the children finally tire of Weezie's Garden,
you could take a stroll through the rest of Elm Bank's
grounds to view the dramatic Italianate and Bressingham Gardens (chapter 11)—but after a wealth
of sensory delights at Weezie's, how could any
child be content to look and not touch?

Dr. Paul Dudley White Charles River Bike Path

www.eot.state.ma.us; Search: Dudley White Bike Path
Open all year, dawn to dusk, ice and snow permitting
Handicap accessible; however, bicyclists may travel at high speeds
Free

Ah, the sparkling Charles! This eighteen-mile loop winds along both sides of the Charles River from Boston's Science Park to Watertown Square.

The path was laid in the 1960s from Science Park to Fresh Pond on the north side of the Charles and to the BU Bridge on the south. It was expanded to its current length in the 1980s. Today, the path's condition varies considerably. Along the Esplanade (chapter 3) and east of the Longfellow Bridge on the Boston side, there are dedicated lanes wide enough for two bicycles to pass; farther upstream, the path is reduced to a narrow strip of pavement barely wide enough for one rider. Despite its shortcomings, it's an invigorating ride.

If you want a wide bike path, pedal over to Memorial Drive in Cambridge. The road is closed from Western Avenue to Mount Auburn Street from 11:00am–7:00pm on Sundays from late April through November.

East Boston Greenway

www.bostonnatural.org/greenways.htm
Open all year, dawn to dusk, ice and snow permitting
Handicap accessible; however, bicyclists may travel at high speeds
Free

Like many other Boston-area bike trails, the East Boston Greenway is a work in progress. One day, the East Boston Greenway will run for 3.3 miles on an abandoned railroad right-of-way from East Boston's Piers Park to Belle Isle Marsh. Today, thanks largely to years of community activism by the Boston Natural Areas Network and the Friends of the East Boston Greenway, the greenway runs roughly from Piers Park in East Boston past the MBTA Maverick Station, through Bremen Street Park past Logan Airport, to Prescott Street; a small portion of the trail is also paved at Constitution Beach. Separate bicycle and walking lanes make travel through the park easier on everyone's nerves.

The existing route makes for a pleasant urban ride. South Bremen Street, where the trail begins at a blue caboose, has a typical East Boston mix of streamlined new development, abandoned piers and buildings, and nineteenth-century triple-decker houses stuffed cheek by jowl from street corner to street corner. Bremen Street Park itself is a pleasant new eighteen-acre city park (opened in 2008) with young trees, a playground, bocce court,

amphitheater, community garden, and sprinklers for children. However, keep in mind that the long axis of this linear park runs by the Route 1A and Massachusetts Turnpike entrances to Logan Airport. It's a fascinating place as long as you don't expect much peace and quiet.

While you're in the area, stop by the Joe Ciampa Community Garden at the corner of Cottage Avenue and Marginal Street. A winner of a Boston Mayor's Garden Contest award for community gardening, the small garden hosts what must be the largest, most lovingly tended outdoor fig tree in the Boston area.

South Bay Harbor Trail

www.southbaytrail.com
Open all year dawn to dusk, ice and snow permitting
Handicap accessible; however, bicyclists may travel at high speeds
Free

Work has just begun on the South Bay Harbor Trail, a 3.5-mile bicycle and walking path running from Fan Pier on the Boston Harbor to the MBTA Ruggles Station in the South End.

The planned route follows the existing Boston Harborwalk (chapter 2) south from Fan Pier along the Fort Point Channel to South Boston's Broadway Street Bridge. After crossing the bridge, travelers can continue along Albany Street to Massachusetts Avenue, then go west along Melnea Cass Boulevard to Ruggles. Bicyclists looking to extend their rides can cycle up Ruggles Street past the Museum of Fine Arts to the Fens, part of Boston's Emerald Necklace (chapter 1). The trail will be marked with salvaged buoys and historical signs shaped like sails on a

mast. Path users will also have access to bike racks, showers, and lockers at Fan Pier. Construction of the path is expected to be complete in late 2010.

Apart from wonderful views and a new connection between Boston neighborhoods and the sea, the South Bay Harbor Trail is notable as an example of public-nonprofit collaboration. The city of Boston has been working with Save the Harbor/Save the Bay to plan the trail since Mayor Tom Menino announced the city's support on Earth Day 2001. Save the Harbor/Save the Bay raised almost $1 million for the project, which the state matched with $3.9 million in federal highway funds. Now, the long, hard work of planning and cooperation is finally paying off. Enjoy the trail, and be grateful for Boston's city spirit.

Neponset River Greenway

617-727-5290
www.mass.gov/dcr; Search: Neponset River Trail
Open all year, dawn to dusk, ice and snow permitting
Handicap accessible; however, bicyclists may travel at high speeds
Free

This 2.5-mile path runs along the Neponset River from Tenean Beach on Tenean Street, Dorchester, through Pope John Paul II and Neponset Parks. From there, the path follows the old railroad right-of-way past the Neponset River Reservation marshes, and then takes an inland route following the MBTA Red Line tracks past Butler Station to Central Avenue. The marsh views are particularly soothing—different from the broad river vistas and close-built cityscape. Along the route are several bright murals by the

Boston Natural Area Network's Youth Conservation Corps.

The Neponset River Greenway Council envisions the path one day extending to Mattapan Square, then following the river again to a link trail to Blue Hills Reservation (chapter 16). This day may not be far off: in April 2008, state officials announced funding of $5.2 million to build the Neponset River Esplanade between Mattapan Square and Hyde Park, including a 2.5-mile-long bike path that would end near the Blue Hills.

Minuteman Bikeway

MBTA Alewife Station to Depot Park/South Street, Bedford
www.minutemanbikeway.org
Open daily, 5:00AM–9:00PM, ice and snow permitting
Handicap accessible; however, bicyclists may travel at high speeds
Free

The Minuteman Bikeway is hands-down the most popular bicycle path in Greater Boston—and one of the most traveled in America. It's estimated that more than two million visitors traveling between Cambridge, Arlington, Lexington, and Bedford enjoy this 10.4-mile path each year. It's useful for commuters who travel via the MBTA, as it provides off-street transportation. What's more, the bikeway traverses some of these suburbs' most beautiful open spaces.

Ride west on the Minuteman, and you'll see Arlington's Spy Pond, the Great Meadows in Lexington, and Lexington's Parker Meadow. Other parks, like the Arlington Reservoir, are just a few blocks away, as are ice cream shops in Arlington and Lexington Centers. Frequent access points mean that riders can stop and find whatever they need from anywhere on the route. Even better, much of the bike path is shaded by trees that grew up after the railroad line was abandoned. It's a leafy, green ride. It's also very crowded on sunny weekend afternoons, when bicyclists, joggers, walkers, and in-line skaters head for the path. If you'd prefer a solitary ride, it's best to start going west beyond Lexington Center.

The path is a twelve-foot-wide strip of pavement owned by the MBTA. The Minuteman Bikeway was first proposed in 1974, while an anemic commuter rail line was still functioning on the right-of-way. After the railroad was finally abandoned in 1977, it took advocates another fifteen years to get government approval and funds to establish the path on the abandoned railroad. They persisted, and the path was built from Bedford to Arlington in 1991–1993. An extension from East Arlington to Alewife Station was built in 1998. From Alewife, travelers can continue on the Linear Path to Somerville.

Battle Road Trail

Old Massachusetts Avenue at Wood Street (Ebenezer Fiske House Site), Lexington, to Meriam's Corner, Concord
978-369-6993
www.nps.gov/mima; Search: Battle Road Trail
Open all year, dawn to dusk, ice and snow permitting
Handicap accessible; however, bicyclists may travel at high speeds
Free

LEFT: MINUTEMAN BIKE TRAIL. RIGHT: BATTLE ROAD TRAIL.

Ride through history! The five-mile-long Battle Road Trail is part of the Minute Man National Historic Park and traces the route British troops followed during the Battles of Lexington and Concord on April 19, 1775. Historically inclined visitors can read on trailside markers the sometimes gruesome descriptions of local residents' clashes with the British. Along the way, the trail travels through an 849-acre park, past open farmland and historic houses, and through forests filled with sugar maples, white oaks, and beeches.

Don't ride too quickly. In pleasant weather, visitors from the world over leave the park's visitor center and take to the trail with strollers, wheelchairs, and slow reaction times. Bike carefully.

The Massachusetts Bicycle Coalition

The Massachusetts Bicycle Coalition (Mass Bike) makes life easier for bicyclists—and more fun. Founded in 1977 as the Boston Area Bicycle Coalition, Mass Bike runs group rides, holds classes in bicycle maintenance and safety, lobbies government officials to make roads more bicycle-friendly, and hosts Thirsty Riders Club meetings in Boston pubs.

If you've ever biked on the Minuteman Bikeway, used a bike rack on the street or at an MBTA station, or just ridden on the streets of Boston and survived, you've benefited from Mass Bike's work. Today, Mass Bike continues to advocate for many issues, including bicycle-friendly public transportation and safe routes for children to bike to school, but their members still find time to lead trips like a Halloween bicycle tour of Boston's graveyards.

Take Mass Bike's website out for a spin. You'll find descriptions of Mass Bike's current projects and lists of Boston-area bike paths at massbike.org.

15.   Grand Estates

IF YOU'D LIKE TO STROLL ABOUT A GREAT LAWN WITH A PARASOL admiring roses, venture beyond Boston. Several suburban estates, left to nonprofit groups by the well-intentioned rich of the past, open their pleasure gardens to the public. You may visit their landscapes of delight for a day, often for a fee. Appreciate the venerable cherries at Long Hill; choose seaside excess at Castle Hill, Ipswich; or creep through the medieval courtyard at Hammond Castle. Whatever your fancy, you are sure to be inspired by these beautiful gardens.

LEFT: SHIRLEY EUSTIS HOUSE. ABOVE: LONGFELLOW NATIONAL HISTORIC SITE.

Sedgwick Gardens at Long Hill

572 Essex Street, Beverly
978-921-1944
www.thetrustees.org; Search: Sedgwick Gardens,
Long Hill
Gardens and grounds open daily, dawn to dusk
Not handicap accessible
Free

Have you ever wanted to see seventy-five-year-old flowering cherry trees? Or every possible color of azalea blooming at once around a pointy-roofed gazebo? The Sedgwick Gardens at Long Hill will surely satisfy. The fruit of sixty-three years of garden design by two wealthy women, the Sedgwick Gardens are five acres of distinct spaces in forest clearings decorated with spring flowers. These decorative gardens are full of rhododendrons, azaleas, tree peonies, lilacs, Japanese maples, roses, forsythia, and spring bulbs galore.

Ellery Sedgwick, a writer and editor of the *Atlantic Monthly*, bought Long Hill in 1916 as a summer home for himself and his wife, Mabel Cabot Sedgwick. Mrs. Sedgwick was an accomplished horticulturist and herself an author of a book, *Gardening Month by Month*. She designed and planted the gardens at Long Hill until her death in 1937. The second Mrs. Sedgwick, one Marjorie Russell, was also an amateur horticulturist and added several more exotic species first introduced by the Arnold

Arboretum. Today, the gardens host four hundred species of plants.

Judging by their gardens, both Mesdames Sedgwicks liked to surprise people. The gardens are sprinkled through the woods around the house, so they can't be seen all at once. Instead, they appear as you wander through, discovering the Sedgwicks' taste in statuary: a crane here, an arch there.

Beyond the gardens are another one hundred acres of forest, fields, and orchards, as well as the Food Project's newest farm site. For more information on the Food Project's urban farms, see chapter 10.

Castle Hill

The Crane Estate, Argilla Road, Ipswich
978-356-4351 | www.thetrustees.org
Grounds open daily, 8:00AM–dusk; grounds near the Great House may be closed during private functions
Not handicap accessible
Tours: Historic landscape tours of Castle Hill are on Thursdays and Saturdays, late May–October at 10:00AM. House tours are Wednesdays–Saturdays, late May–October, 10:00AM–1:00PM (one-hour tour)
Admission: Grounds admissions are $2 per bicycle, $4 per motorcycle, $8 per car on weekends and Monday holidays, Memorial Day weekend to Labor Day weekend; $5 per car other times; free for Trustees of Reservations members; discounted 50 percent after 3:00PM. House tours for adults, $10; children over eight, $5; fee includes admission to grounds

A grand house by the seaside, with trails on over 165 acres of forest, grasslands, and dunes—but what you remember is the lawn. The Grand Allée's enormous swath of grass, lined with dark conifers and eerie statues, rolls downhill until it seems to plunge into the sea. If it actually did, there would be plenty of lifeguards to rescue it: adjoining Crane's Beach is one of the most popular swimming spots on the North Shore.

Richard Crane, a plumbing magnate, had two summer homes built on the hilltop site. The first mansion was an Italian villa constructed circa 1910–1912 shortly after Crane bought the property. The Olmsted Brothers designed landscapes for this villa, complete with flower gardens and fountains, and Arthur Shurcliff designed the Grand Allée, or mall, from 1913–1916. Alas, Crane's wife, Florence, detested the house. Crane agreed that if Florence still hated the house after living in it for ten years, he would build her a new one. Florence's resolve never wavered, and in 1928 the villa non grata was torn down and replaced with the current fifty-nine-room mansion. According to all reports, the bathroom fixtures are spectacular, as would befit a plumbing billionaire.

The basic Olmsted design was preserved through all this rebuilding and is in evidence today. The high-maintenance rose garden and garden maze have been dismantled, although the Trustees of Reservations does maintain a small formal garden on the site. Still, the showy stonework that accompanied the more formal plantings remains—steps and terraces, balustrades and forecourts in all manner of places. A former saltwater swimming pool halfway up the Grand Allée has become a frame for turf grass.

Altogether, Castle Hill is an impressive place to frolic in the ruins of the idle rich. For a less civilized experience, visit the abutting Crane Wildlife Refuge, another 697 acres of marshy land with three and a half miles of maintained trails.

Hammond Castle Museum

80 Hesperus Avenue, Gloucester
978-283-2080 | www.hammondcastle.org
Hours and fees vary, closed November–May
Not handicap accessible
Adults, $10; seniors, $8; and children (6–12), $6

In Gloucester, there is a stone castle by the sea, surrounded by small gardens, with a lush courtyard within. The Hammond Castle is certainly one of the most dramatic places in New England—as well as one of the most jumbled museums on the planet. The interior courtyard adds verdant plants to the mix of medieval relics and modern notions.

The Hammond Castle Museum was built by John Hays Hammond Jr., a handy inventor who earned four hundred patents for things like submarine sound transmitters and radio-controlled rockets. Construction took place from 1926 to 1929, but the castle really can't decide what century it's in. The Great Hall is Romanesque; other areas feature Gothic designs or French Renaissance or 1920s New England; the exterior is graced with medieval doorways and Roman-style tombstones.

The courtyard is supposed to mimic a medieval town square built around Roman ruins. The walls facing the courtyard are made up of house fronts Hammond purchased on his journeys, while the center of the space is taken up by a large pool. Potted greenery abounds—ivy, geraniums, and some rather enormous trees—giving the place a tropical air. The center pool is flanked by stone columns, and bits of statuary are scattered among the leaves. The effect of all this ornamentation is either spectacular or ridiculous, depending upon one's tastes.

Outside, the grounds lead to the ocean. The hillside and the castle's foundation are lush, planted with demure sprinklings of rhododendrons, yews, daylilies, and cheerful perennials. The grounds are just about the only simple feature around this place.

Larz Anderson Park

23 Newton Street, Brookline
617-730-2088
www.brooklinema.gov; Search: Larz Anderson Park
Open all year, dawn to dusk
Some facilities handicap accessible
Free

With sweeping views of Boston from atop a high grassy slope, Larz Anderson Park is one of the finest picnic spots and sledding hills in Boston. That hilltop is also a fine site for garden detectives: the remains of several gardens designed by Little and Browne and Charles Platt in the early 1900s are visible—if you know where to look. The low-lying regions of this spacious park include a large shady playground with bathrooms, a large water garden, community garden plots, playing fields, and an historic one-room schoolhouse.

The estate once belonged to Larz Anderson, a diplomat and businessman, who bought the sixty-four-acre property with his wife, Isabel Weld Perkins, in 1899. Their hilltop estate was called Weld, after Isabel's family. Isabel left the property to the town of Brookline in 1948.

Entering from Goddard Avenue, visitors can view a water garden designed in 1910 by Little and Browne with a gazebo most likely copied from the similar Temple of Love structure at Versailles. Nearby is the sole remnant of Little and Browne's Chinese garden: a basin with a lion-head spout hidden amid the brush.

Halfway up the hill from the Newton Street House is a grand mansion that currently houses the Larz Anderson Auto Museum, which contains

fourteen of Anderson's classiest vehicles. When the Andersons lived here, this elegant domicile was a mere carriage house; the Andersons inhabited their own mansion on top of the hill. That stately home was demolished by the town of Brookline in 1955 and is now a parking lot.

At the top of the hill, near the parking lot, are remnants of a bowling green and an Italian garden, both designed by Charles A. Platt. The Italian garden is now a skating rink, watched by the garden's sole remaining statue; the green is a lawn with a low balustrade and a large semi-circular stone bench. A large stone-paved terrace with a stone trellis marks the former front of the Weld mansion. Steps off the terrace lead to what was once a Japanese garden designed by Onchi San, a Japanese gardener Anderson invited to Weld in 1907. All that remains of this garden are a few small stone sculptures with Japanese motifs.

Garden detectives will want to download a map titled "Rediscover Weld at Larz Anderson Park" from the resources section of the Brookline Green Space Alliance website, brooklinegreenspace.org. Children will want to alternate between romping at the spiffy playground and running themselves silly on that wonderful, wide-open hill.

Longfellow National Historic Site

105 Brattle Street, Cambridge
617-876-4491 | www.nps.gov/long

LONGFELLOW NATIONAL HISTORIC SITE.

Spring–fall, gardens and grounds open dawn to dusk; call for house tour schedule
Grounds, visitor center, carriage house, and first floor of house handicap-accessible
No fee to tour grounds and gardens; house entrance fee is $3 for ages sixteen and up

*Listen my children and you shall hear
Of the midnight ride of Paul Revere.*

Henry Wadsworth Longfellow, poet and Harvard professor, was the author of many notable poems, including "Paul Revere's Ride" and "The Song of Hiawatha." However, his daughter Alice's genius shone in her garden, which became a nationally known Colonial revival landscape under her care from 1882 to 1928.

Today, the site features smooth lawns, disease-resistant elms, and Alice's resplendent formal garden, restored and replanted in 2005–2006 with over two thousand perennial plants and seventeen hundred boxwood shrubs, as well as lilacs, roses, and bush honeysuckle, hollies, serviceberries, pines, and junipers.

The Longfellow property is the remnant of a much larger Colonial estate—a 6.5-acre house lot abutting ninety acres of farmlands, orchards, and hay fields. In 1759, John Vassall built a Georgian-style house on the property. The Loyalist Vassalls fled Boston in 1775 in anticipation of war, and George Washington took up residence in their stately home for nine months in 1775–1776 during the Siege of Boston. Over time, the house was improved and excess land sold off. The Craigie family took over the house in 1791. The Craigies were intrigued by horticulture; they built greenhouses and donated three acres of their land to Harvard University for a botanic garden. The house and five acres of land were given to Henry Wadsworth Longfellow as a wedding present in 1843.

Longfellow enjoyed gardening. His daughter Alice wrote, "He was much interested in planting new trees and shrubs and laying out an old fashioned garden. The plan of the somewhat elaborate flower beds was his own design, surrounded by low borders of box[wood] and filled with flowers." He enjoyed the view of the Charles and the house's signature elms which framed the front lawn and lilacs.

Longfellow died in 1882, and Alice took over the home. In 1904, Alice hired Martha Brooks Hutcheson, the first female landscape architect in the United States, to overhaul the property. Hutcheson created a Colonial revival garden atop the remnants of Henry Wadsworth Longfellow's stylized flower beds. At the time, Colonial revival gardens were an attempt to recreate grandmother's garden. Based on romantic ideas of Colonial life as much as the sketchy records of Colonial-era horticulture, these gardens are formal, planned with straight lines extending from house to garden. The plants are old-fashioned and loosely pruned; the Longfellow garden featured plants like lilacs, old roses, lavender, and phlox. Hutcheson framed the beds with boxwood and installed a pergola and lattice fence inspired by Colonial-era architecture.

In 1925, Alice Longfellow hired landscape architect Ellen Biddle Shipman to renew the landscape, which had become tired and overgrown. Shipman did not alter Hutcheson's basic design. Instead, she replanted the Longfellows' favorite flowers, then expanded the garden in three dimensions. She added rectangular rose beds as borders and planted columnar arborvitae, ornamental cherries, and dwarf crabapple trees to raise the garden's borders toward the sky. The restored garden largely recapitulates Hutcheson's redesign, which was amply documented.

Today, the formal garden features heritage varieties of several species, especially asters and garden phlox, among the two thousand heirloom perennials, three hundred heirloom annuals, and nearly eleven hundred tulips, daffodils, dahlias, and gladiola bulbs planted on the site. The place is filled with blooms across the growing seasons, full of wonders and worthy of Henry Wadsworth Longfellow's lines in his poem "Flowers":

Wondrous truths, and manifold as wondrous,
God hath written in those stars above;
But not less in the bright flowerets under us
Stands the revelation of his love.

Alice Longfellow was also a patron of learning: Longfellow Hall at the nearby Radcliffe Institute is named for her. The institute grounds feature sculptures and a sunken garden; stroll over to Garden Street by Appian Way to see it.

Shirley Eustis House Garden and Orchard

33 Shirley Street, Roxbury
617-442-2275 | www.shirleyeustishouse.org
House tours available June 1–September 30, Thursday, Friday, and second weekend of the month, noon–4:00PM
House not accessible; outdoor paths covered with gravel or mulch
House admission is $5 for adults, $3 for children under twelve and seniors

When the royal governor of Massachusetts Bay Colony strolled his mansion's grounds, he could survey thirty-three acres of rural estate. Today, the Shirley Eustis House stands on a modest lot in thickly settled Roxbury. The garden plantings are simple yet formal, as befits an official residence, and feature white urns, ivy, and a small gazebo. Earthworks Boston has planted thirty heirloom fruit trees on the property, along with antique varieties of currants and gooseberries.

The house itself was built in Georgian style from 1741 to 1751 by Colonial governor William Shirley, appointed by King George II. It has been restored to reflect its Federal period furnishings and to preserve the house's staircases and moldings; only the library is Georgian today.

Today, the Shirley Eustis House overlooks a broad lawn divided by a narrow linear garden bed featuring perennials, Scotch briar roses, and hydrangeas. The front of the lawn features a circle of pavement surrounding a bed of English ivy and a raised white urn planted with trailing greenery. The rear lawn has a garden gazebo that was once a cupola in Louis Cabot's Brookline mansion.

Earthworks' heirloom fruit trees are planted along the property's southern border and in a small orchard across Rockford Street. The plantings include five Roxbury russet apple trees, scions of trees bred in Boston prior to 1650. A fine dessert apple, the Roxbury russets are prized for winter storage and for making hard cider. Visitors are free to pick and eat the apples in season—a taste of Boston's past. Be aware that these authentic heirloom trees are organically grown and can be marked with apple scab and other unflattering tree diseases.

Apart from the russets, Earthworks has installed ten apple trees, nine pears, two nectarines, two apricots, two peaches, four cherries, a plum, nine currant bushes, and four gooseberry bushes. Enjoy the taste of history.

SHIRLEY EUSTIS HOUSE GARDEN AND ORCHARD.

The Trustees of Reservations

They won't book you dinner or theater tickets. Instead, the Trustees of Reservations preserves and protects more than twenty four thousand acres of gardens, land, and historic houses in Massachusetts.

The Trustees was created in 1891 by Charles Eliot, a nineteenth-century landscape architect who also helped create the Charles River Esplanade.

The Trustees' first land purchase that year was the twenty-acre Virginia Woods in Stoneham, now part of the Middlesex Fells. Today, the Trustees owns and oversees ninety-nine different sites in Massachusetts, ranging from homes once inhabited by Henry David Thoreau or Herman Melville to working farms, waterfalls, gardens, early industrial sites, and properties

with strong ties to Native American history. The Trustees also work to help other organizations protect land via workshops and conferences led by the Trustees' Putnam Conservation Institute.

If you'd like to learn more about Massachusetts's historic landscapes, visit any one of the many sites or go online: www.thetrustees.org.

16.   Suburban Wilderness

SOMETIMES YOU JUST WANT TO RUN WILD. WITHIN TEN MILES of Boston there are thousands of acres of reservations, forested land that is largely left untouched. With the exception of Stony Brook Reservation, parks within Boston's city limits have been completely transformed by human activity. But beyond Boston, and in Stony Brook, visitors can observe several natural communities. Three of the most common natural communities in Boston-area wilds are oak-hickory forests on upland slopes, acidic rocky summits, and red maple swamps in muddy, mushy lowlands.

Oak-hickory forest is the natural community you will find in the dry acid soil of most Boston-area suburban parks and hillsides. Oaks predominate, with a few hickories sprinkled in. Smaller trees include sassafras, shadbush, and witch hazel. You'll find plenty of low-bush blueberries in these forests, along with maple-leaf viburnums and smaller plants, like wild sarsaparilla

LEFT: MIDDLESEX FELLS. ABOVE: WORLD'S END, PART OF THE BOSTON HARBOR ISLANDS NATIONAL PARK AREA.

and tick trefoil. Wild turkeys thrive on the acorns, as do chipmunks, white-footed mice, red-eyed vireos, and scarlet tanagers.

Acidic rocky summit communities are sparse, open places on rocky hilltops with scattered low shrubs, grasses, lichens, and a few small trees. Pitch pines or red oaks may grow along the margins, but the most common woody plants in these communities are scrub oaks, huckleberries, blueberries, chokecherries, and serviceberries. Little bluestem grass grows here, and pink and yellow pale corydalis flowers are cheerful summer blooms. Various rodents and ravens visit these sites but don't make their homes in these exposed, windy places.

Red maple swamps are the most common wetlands plant community in Massachusetts. Red maples make up the overstory, along with a mix of

trees that can include swamp white oak, hemlock, or black gum. The shrub layer in these swamps is often dominated by scented sweet pepperbush and the bright blooms of swamp azalea as well as highbush blueberries. The moist soils support plenty of ferns and skunk cabbage, marsh marigolds and bugleweed. Before the swamps' vernal pools dry up in the summer, they provide valuable spring breeding habitat for salamanders, frogs, and other species that don't care to have fish eating their eggs. However, even year-round pools are home to plenty of frogs.

MIDDLE BREWSTER ISLAND.

Convenient and underused, these suburban wildernesses are easy places to get away from the city for a few hours. Hike through the forests at Stony Brook and Beaver Brook North Reservations; lose yourself in the acres of the Middlesex Fells; climb the Great Blue Hill in Milton; marvel at North Shore boulders and foliage at the Lynn Woods and Breakheart Reservation; and enjoy the solitude—then walk back out to the bus stop.

Boston Harbor Islands

Ferry from Long Wharf, Boston, and piers in South Boston, Quincy, Hingham, and Hull
617-223-8666 | www.bostonislands.org
Ferry service is available May–November
Some islands handicap accessible
Ferry ticket costs vary

They're far away yet so close. A ferry ride from Long Wharf will bring you to fifteen hundred acres of park land on thirty-four islands scattered through Boston Harbor. They're all part of a national park area and all within ten miles of Boston. Some are wild places with little more than thickets and marshes and pebbly beaches; others sport summer cottages, concrete bunkers, an historic fort, the ruins of grand estates, and lighthouses.

Today, the first two ferry stops from Long Wharf are Georges Island and Spectacle Island. Spectacle Island, a former landfill that was supposedly so foul smelling that ships in foggy weather could navigate by the stench, has been capped with 3.5 million cubic yards of material excavated when the Ted Williams Tunnel and other roadways were constructed. Today, it's a 105-acre park with a swimming beach, a high drumlin-top with panoramic views of Boston,

meadows home to more than one hundred bird species, and a visitor center with a cafe.

Georges Island is a low-slung thirty-nine acres dominated by Fort Warren, a mid-nineteenth-century fort that served as a Civil War prison. The fort really is a warren of rooms with intriguing ceiling brickwork and a few explanatory signs. Children and acrophiles will enjoy walking on top of the fort's walls to see views of Boston. The island also hosts a small snack bar, picnic tables, and meadows. Georges Island is also the Harbor Islands' ferry hub; change here to travel on to less-frequented islands.

Beyond Spectacle and Georges Islands, visitors can reserve primitive camp sites on rustic Bumpkin, Lovells, or Grape Islands or admire rare seaside goldenrods at Peddocks Island. Special ferries run directly to Little Brewster. If you aren't sure of your sea legs, venture to World's End, a peninsula "island" reachable by car. Ferry service changes throughout the year; check with park management to confirm times.

Stony Brook Reservation

Turtle Pond Parkway, West Roxbury/Hyde Park
617-333-7404 | www.mass.gov/dcr; Search:
Stony Brook Reservation
Open all seasons, dawn to dusk
Handicap accessible restrooms, playground
Free

The 1898 edition of *Walks and Rides in the Country Round About Boston* described Stony Brook Reservation as "a tract of striking beauty, embracing 475 acres of rolling and rocky woodland, highland, and swamps." Stony Brook hasn't changed much since then. Founded in 1894, Stony Brook Reservation is still 475 acres of woods inside Boston's city limits. Most of that land is oak-hickory forest: white and red oak trees interspersed with hickories and white pines. Understory plants include shorter sassafras, witch hazel, and cherry trees, maple-leaf viburnums, and the ever popular poison ivy.

There are twelve paved paths and rustic walking trails in the park, with some poorly marked and confusing intersections; print out a map from the website before you go. Many of these trails range over the park's elevation from 15 to 338 feet above sea level. Blueberries, huckleberries, and bear oaks grow on exposed hilltops. Numerous

ledge outcroppings and glacial erratic boulders will satisfy most visitors yearning to see big rocks. The reservation also has extensive wetlands around Turtle Pond and other low-lying areas of the park, primarily red maple swamps. The combination of hilly, forested terrain and mud is probably why the park escaped being converted into farmland centuries ago. Other facilities include a playground, soccer fields, and tennis courts in the southern and eastern edges of the park, but the largest portion of the park is crisscrossed by paved paths and old fire roads through forest.

The most visited—or at least most photographed—site in Stony Brook is Turtle Pond. In the fall, the maples by the pond ignite in fiery color. However lovely those inflamed hues, amateur botanists will seek out a more subtle arboreal phenomenon: a small grove of mature American chestnut trees. More than four billion American chestnut trees, a quarter of the hardwood forest trees in the eastern United States, were killed by chestnut blight in the twentieth century. These trees are some of the few survivors. The American Chestnut Foundation carefully pollinates these trees and harvests the burrs in the fall for their work breeding a blight-resistant American chestnut tree. If you see tractor-tire tracks nearby, they were probably left by the cherry-picker trucks Massachusetts utility companies loan to the foundation to tend to the trees.

The pond is also the source of the Stony Brook, more accurately the Stony Brook Conduit nowadays. The river was covered and contained in the late 1800s and early 1900s to control flooding, from about a mile upstream of Turtle Pond to its mouth at the Charles River.

If, for some reason, you choose not to leave your car when you arrive at Stony Brook, do yourself the favor of driving around the reservation. Eight parkways designed by the Olmsted Brothers surround

and pass through the reservation and are listed on the National Register of Historic Places.

Stony Brook Reservation also has five miles of paved bicycle paths crisscrossing its acres of hilly oak-hickory forest.

Beaver Brook North Reservation

290 Mill Street (Rock Meadow), Belmont
617-484-6357 (Department of Conservation and Recreation)
www.mass.gov/dcr; Search: Beaver Brook
Open all year, dawn to dusk
Not handicap accessible; trails are covered in dirt, grass, or stones
Free

Habitat Education Center and Wildlife Sanctuary, 10 Juniper Road, Belmont
617-489-5050 (Audubon)
www.massaudubon.org; Search: Habitat
Habitat Education Center open Monday–Friday, 8:00AM–4:00PM; Saturday and Sunday, 10:00AM–4:00PM
Nature Center, Garden Terrace, and restrooms are handicap accessible
Adults, $4; children (3–12) and seniors, $3; children under three and Massachusetts Audubon members, free

Tucked away behind all the charming homes and minor highways of Belmont, Waltham, and Lexington is three hundred acres of astonishingly well-preserved forest, in a state reservation so new that it almost seems secret. Here you'll find trails through woodlands and wetlands, old carriage roads, open meadows, and small glacial ridges called eskers—if you can find the place at all. In the first three years since the Department of Conservation and Recreation acquired the property, no trail maps were published, and its entrances are currently unmarked. The place also shares a name with neighboring Beaver Brook Reservation, a charming but much smaller and more civilized fifty-nine-acre park.

Until 2006, Beaver Brook North was better known as the grounds of the Metropolitan State Hospital, an institution built about 1930 to house Massachusetts's severely mentally ill. In more recent decades, the state began transferring residents out of large psychiatric hospitals to smaller community-based settings, and the hospital closed in 1992. After lengthy negotiations between community residents and various state agencies, a developer purchased the twenty-three-acre hospital site at the top of the hill to build a 387-unit apartment complex; the rest of the land has remained open space as a shady forest.

Today, hikers can find a wealth of ecosystems on-site. Beaver Brook is primarily oak-hickory forest, but visitors can also find cattail marshes, red maple swamps, open meadows, and vernal pools complete with fairy shrimp, a small crustacean. There's even a quaking bog, where mats of vegetation are forming over a small pond in the West Meadow at the end of Marguerite Terrace, Waltham.

Beaver Brook North is a relatively stable property for native plants. Most of the land has been undisturbed for decades, and invasive species like Asiatic bittersweet, buckthorn, garlic mustard, and Norway maples have not taken over Beaver Brook the way they've infested other local sites. The large interior forest encourages many species that don't adapt well to strips of land next to urban development. Great horned owls breed here, as do dozens of other bird species, wood frogs, and painted turtles. American woodcocks mate in the grasslands at adjoining Rock Meadow. The birds also put on impressive aeronautic displays in March.

Beaver Brook North is part of a larger network of open space called the Western Greenway, a six-mile-long loop of open green space circling through Belmont, Lexington, and Waltham. Navigating the space can be confusing even though volunteers are hard at work putting up trail markers and building boardwalks to clarify the connections between Rock Meadow and Beaver Brook North. Stop by and pick up information about the greenway from the staff at Belmont's Massachusetts Audubon Sanctuary; if there's a Beaver Brook North trail map, they'll know.

Middlesex Fells

Malden, Medford, Stoneham, Melrose, and Winchester
617-727-5380
www.mass.gov/dcr; Search: Fells
781-662-2340 | www.fells.org
Open all year, dawn to dusk
Not handicap accessible
Free

Feeling like you need more space? How would two thousand and sixty acres suit you? A quick spin up Route 93 brings visitors to this mammoth landscape of rocky hills, wetlands, oak-hickory forests, meadows, ponds, vernal pools, blueberries, whitetail deer, lady slipper orchids, blue spotted salamanders, and just about anything else you might want to find in the woods. Miles and miles of trails include a special off-road mountain biking loop, a hike to a three-story tower, and a nature trail with marked observation stations. The Friends of the Middlesex Fells have pages and pages of

hikes and information about the park's natural history at www.fells.org.

"Fells" is a word for a landscape with rocky hills. Native Americans hunted here for centuries before European colonization. When Europeans arrived, they used the Fells for farming and harvesting wood; the Fells has plenty of old stone walls that marked the boundaries between properties. From about 1830 to 1870, the land was quarried for gravel along the aptly named Quarry Road. Some of its production went into paths in the Boston Common and Public Garden.

The park was assembled by the newly formed Metropolitan Parks Commission in the 1890s. Landscape architect Charles Eliot designed parkways that cross the Fells, and more than five hundred thousand trees were planted on the site in the 1920s to decorate the place and protect the area's reservoirs from erosion. Various recreational complexes were built as the century went on—the Stone Zoo, a swimming pool, a skating rink. Alas, in the 1960s, the construction of Route 93 sliced the Fells in half and isolated wildlife populations.

Today, the Fells is a mix of vast forest spaces and great vistas over an eight-lane highway. You'll find relative peace and quiet walking near Bellevue Pond on South Border Road, but hikers heading for the Bear Hill observation tower will have plenty of company. There is no typical experience in such an enormous place; that's part of the charm.

Blue Hills Reservation

Reservation Headquarters, 695 Hillside Street, Milton
617-698-1802
www.mass.gov/dcr; Search: Blue Hills
Reservation open all seasons, dawn to dusk
Visitor center, restrooms, some trails handicap-accessible; all-terrain wheelchairs available
Free

Blue Hills Trailside Museum, 1904 Canton Avenue, Milton
617-333-0690
www.massaudubon.org; Search: Blue Hills
Call for museum hours
Nature center and restrooms are handicap accessible
Call for museum admission fees

This 7,000-acre park is big enough to hold a museum, a swimming beach, a seasonal camp for the Appalachian Mountain Club, a boardwalk through a bog, a golf course, and 125 miles of trails and still has room for a 635-foot mountain—Great Blue Hill, one of twenty-two hills in the park.

The Metropolitan Parks Commission did the world a favor when it bought this tract of logged forest and granite outcrops in 1893. The commission created the parkways through the reservation but left most of the interior untouched. The Civilian Conservation Corps built many of the Blue Hills' trails, two stone observation towers, and other facilities in the 1930s. Since then, the Blue Hills have stayed pretty much intact, and pretty much wild—unlike the Middlesex Fells.

Like many other Boston-area forests, the Blue Hills are mostly oak-hickory forest, with blueberries and huckleberries sprinkled on rocky hilltops—but there

exhibits on the history and geology of the site as well as local wildlife. From there, you can climb to the top of Great Blue Hill for panoramic views of Boston, then continue on the popular Skyline Trail along the tops of all the lesser hills in the reservation—all twenty-two of them, if you have the time.

Lynn Woods

Pennybrook Road, Lynn
781-477-7123
www.ci.lynn.ma.us; Search: Lynn Woods
Open all year, dawn to dusk. Dungeon Rock open May–October, 9:00AM–2:30PM; call to confirm
Not handicap accessible
Free

are several other environments in this vast tract as well. For example the Ponkapoag Bog, a quaking bog of mats of vegetation atop a pond, hosts carnivorous sundews and pitcher plants. Visitors can reach the bog via a deteriorating, slippery cedar plank boardwalk (bring waterproof boots or a second pair of shoes and socks). The two hundred-acre Ponkapoag Pond, as opposed to the bog, is a fine place for canoeing. If you'd like to see fish, Houghton's Pond is stocked with trout, and sunfish lurk in the Marigold Marsh nearby.

To get a sense of the place, start your visit at the Massachusetts Audubon Society's Blue Hills Trailside Museum located at the foot of Great Blue Hill. The museum has a relief map of the reservation and

Not to be outdone by Boston, the North Shore city of Lynn has a 2,200-acre forest within city limits. Founded in 1881, the Lynn Woods is one of the largest city parks in the United States and covers one-fifth of Lynn. The site is very popular with mountain bikers, but there are plenty of forested trails for everyone, as well as a rose garden, a five-story-tall stone tower, and—perhaps—pirate gold!

The woods are primarily oak-hickory-white pine forest, with pitch pine, bear oak, and blueberries on exposed hilltops. Walden Pond (no, not that Walden Pond, chapter 3) roughly divides the woods into two sections. The southern portion of the park is where visitors will find many of the Lynn Woods's most famous features: Lynn Park Superintendent John Morrissey first cultivated the Lynn Woods Rose Garden in the 1920s, and it has undergone several periods of neglect and restoration since then. Closer to the pond is the forty-eight-foot-tall rustic stone fire observation tower constructed by the Work Progress

Administration in 1936 atop Burrill Hill. Dungeon Rock, by the shore of Breed's Pond, supposedly contains the treasure of a band of pirates who appeared in Lynn in 1658. Almost two centuries later, convinced that they could communicate with the dead, a family of Spiritualists named Marble arrived and dug strange wavering tunnels into the rock for twenty-two years in a quixotic quest for treasure. Lynn lost its Marbles when the family's only son died in 1880. The entrance to Dungeon Rock is sealed with an iron grating, but intrepid souls can venture inside during opening hours and see just as much treasure as the Marbles ever did.

To the north of Walden Pond the terrain is increasingly rocky, with many boulders and exposed rock faces. Mountain bikers adore the place; hikers will either be delighted or annoyed at scrambling over the rocks, which can become quite slippery when wet. Amateur geologists will enjoy Balanced Boulder, and fine views can be had from Weetamoo Cliff.

For even more rocky fun—or a dip in a lake, as no swimming is allowed in Lynn Woods—visit the Breakheart Reservation two miles away.

Breakheart Reservation

177 Forest Street, Saugus
781-233-0834
www.mass.gov/dcr; Search: Breakheart Reservation
Open all year, dawn to dusk
Visitor center, restrooms; full-access nature trail under construction; all-terrain wheelchairs available
Free

Like the nearby Lynn Woods, the 640-acre Breakheart Reservation is mostly mixed oak-hickory-white pine forest with rocky outcroppings. Unlike the Lynn Woods, Breakheart Reservation is run by the Massachusetts Department of Conservation and Recreation. There's a swimming beach on Pearce Lake in summer months; in fall months, shutterbugs photograph the brilliant foliage reflected in the water here. Plenty of 200- to 300-foot hills provide views of the forest. Breakheart Reservation also has the distinction of being the home of Bark Place, an off-leash area for dogs.

The reservation was donated to the state by Lynn attorney Benjamin Johnson. Johnson had bought several parcels of land to use as a hunting and fishing preserve in the late nineteenth century and left it to the state in 1900. The Civilian Conservation Corps worked on the reservation's roads in the 1930s. Today, the park has nine miles of trails, including three miles of paved paths, and a visitor center.

OPPOSITE: BREAKHEART RESERVATION.

Annual Events

January
Seafarer's Island Holiday, Boston Harbor Islands
www.bostonislands.org

February
Camellias bloom at the Lyman
Estate Greenhouses
www.historicnewengland.org
Mush the Greenways Dog Sled Races
www.bostonnatural.org

March
Boston Natural Areas Network
Gardeners Gathering
www.bostonnatural.org
Maple Sugar Days
www.mass.gov/dcr

April
City Farm Fest (The Food Project)
www.thefoodproject.org
Earth Day park cleanups—various organizations
Spring Herb Sale, Lyman Estate Greenhouses (may take place in early May)
www.historicnewengland.org
Spring Orchid Sale, Lyman Estate Greenhouses
www.historicnewengland.org

May
Duckling Day Parade (Mother's
Day), The Public Garden (Boston)
www.friendsofthepublicgarden.org
Hidden Gardens of Beacon Hill Tour
www.beaconhillgardenclub.org
Lilac Sunday (Mother's Day), Arnold Arboretum
www.arboretum.harvard.edu
Mother's Day Lilac Weekend, Longfellow National Historic Site
www.nps.gov/long/index.htm
Perennial Sale, Lyman Estate Greenhouses
www.historicnewengland.org
Spring Planting Festival and Perennial Divide
www.bostonnatural.org

June–August
During the summer, dozens of programs
are held each week in Boston's parks and
gardens, including outdoor movie nights,
garden tours, festivals, wildlife programs,
and more. For updated listings, check
Boston.com or any of the following sites:

Boston Natural Areas Network
www.bostonnatural.org
Boston Parks Department
www.cityofboston.gov/parks
Historic New England
www.historicnewengland.org
Massachusetts Audubon Society
www.massaudubon.org

Massachusetts Department of
Conservation and Recreation
www.mass.gov/dcr
The Neponset River Greenway Festival
www.bostonnatural.org
Rose Fitzgerald Kennedy Greenway Conservancy
www.rosekennedygreenway.org
The Massachusetts Federation of Farmers Markets
www.massfarmersmarkets.org
Trustees of Reservations
www.thetrustees.org

June
Cape Ann Garden Festival
www.sargenthouse.org
Garden Affairs Tour (Concord)
www.concordmuseum.org
Hosta Sale, Lyman Estate Greenhouses
www.historicnewengland.org
National Trails Day park
clean-ups—various organizations
Secret Gardens of Cambridge Tour
www.cambridgepubliclibrary.org
South End Garden Tour
www.southendgardentour.org

July
Forest Hills Cemetery Lantern Festival
www.foresthillstrust.org

August
Kites on the [Neponset] River
www.bostonnatural.org

September
Fall Harvest and Perennial Divide
www.bostonnatural.org
Fenway Victory Gardens Fensfest
fenwayvictorygardens.com
Massachusetts Open Garden
Days (Carlisle/Lexington)
gardenconservancy.org

October
Angino Farm Harvest Festival
www.newtoncommunityfarm.org
Annual Great Pumpkin Float
www.bostonnatural.org
Fall Orchid Sale, Lyman Estate Greenhouses
www.historicnewengland.org

November
Day of the Dead at Forest Hills Cemetery
www.foresthillstrust.org

December
First Night Boston
www.firstnight.org
Winter Lights Along the East Boston Greenway
www.bostonnatural.org

Where to Learn More

The following organizations offer courses in horticulture, botany, landscaping, agriculture, and other green topics.

The Arnold Arboretum
www.arboretum.harvard.edu
The Boston Natural Areas Network
www.bostonnatural.org
The Food Project
www.thefoodproject.org
The Massachusetts Horticultural Society
www.masshort.org
The New England Wild Flower Society
www.newfs.org
The Northeast Organic Farming Association Massachusetts Chapter
www.nofamass.org

Beyond Boston: Green Space Groups in Massachusetts

These statewide groups and agencies are excellent places to research your next hike, garden visit, or apple-picking expedition. All of them work with multiple sites in Massachusetts—and in some cases all of New England.

Appalachian Mountain Club
www.outdoors.org
Historic New England
www.historicnewengland.org
Massachusetts Audubon Society
www.massaudubon.org
Massachusetts Department of Conservation and Recreation
www.mass.gov/dcr
The Massachusetts Federation of Farmers Markets
www.massfarmersmarkets.org
Trustees of Reservations
www.thetrustees.org

Acknowledgements

Many kind people took the time to share their visions of Boston's green spaces with me. In particular, I'd like to thank Joanne Stanway, Boston Natural Areas Network: Chris Green, Halvorson Design Partnership; Suzanne Taylor, Boston Parks and Recreation: Donna Clark, ReVision House; Jane Hirshi, CitySprouts; The Food Project; Earthworks Boston; Greg Maslowe, Angino Farm; and the reference staff at the Honan Allston Branch Library, who still aren't tired of answering questions about their beautiful building and courtyard. Professor David Marchant was kind enough to help me with glacial terminology at a moment's notice. Nancy Seasholes overwhelmed me with her generosity. She improved this book immeasurably by reviewing the manuscript with keen eyes and sharing her profound knowledge of Boston's landscape and the history of local land-making. I also appreciated Karl Haglund's critical reading and concern for accuracy.

Thanks as well to Xiao "Sherman" Gong for his beautiful photographs, and to Patricia King Powers, who shot the majority of the sites listed in this book and brought these places to life with her wonderful photographs, and to Elizabeth Lawrence for her inspired design of this beautiful book. Also thank you to the staff and interns at Union Park Press: Jossie Auerbach, James Duggan, Corey Major, Erin Whinnery, and Madeline Williams.

I would also like to thank Albert LaFarge, my indefatigable agent. Finally, I'd like to think Nicole Vecchiotti, my patient, energetic publisher, who has taken my mere words and created a beautiful book.

Photo Credits

Jossie Auerbach
Pages: 30; 76; 85; 116; 123; 171.

Xiao "Sherman" Gong
Pages: iii; xvii; 18; 24, top; 27; 36–37; 38; 47; 50; 51; 55; 59, top; 60–61; 108; 109; 110–111; 128, bottom; 144; 146–147; 158-159; 160; 188–189.

Patricia King Powers
Pages: i; vi-viii; xiii, xiv, xvi; 20; 23; 24, bottom left and right; 26; 31; 33; 35; 40; 41; 48; 52; 54; 56; 59, bottom; 63; 67; 70; 71; 72; 74; 79; 80; 82–83; 86; 88; 89; 90; 92; 96; 99; 100; 101; 103; 106; 113; 114; 118; 122; 124; 125; 127; 129; 130; 131; 132; 134; 136; 137; 139; 142; 145; 149; 150; 151; 152; 153; 155; 157; 161; 163; 164; 166; 167; 168; 170; 175; 176; 180; 183; 185; 190–191.

Nicole Vecchiotti/Union Park Press
Pages: ix; 19; 21; 28; 46; 49; 66; 68; 69; 77; 78; 120; 121; 128, top; 156; 172; 177; 178; 179; 187.

Additional photos:
Pages: 44, top and bottom, Margot Anne Kelley; 98, City of Cambridge; 104, City of Cambridge. Map on page 10 by Elizabeth Lawrence.